DR MICHAELA GLÖCKLER has been Leader of the Medical Section at the Goetheanum, the School of Spiritual Science in Dornach, Switzerland, since 1988. She attended the Waldorf School in Stuttgart, then studied German language, literature, and history in Freiburg and Heidelberg. She studied medicine in Tübingen and Marburg and trained as a pediatrician at the community hospital in Herdecke and at the Bochum University Pediatric Clinic. Until 1988 she was a colleague in the children's outpatient clinic at the Community Hospital in Herdecke and served as school doctor for the Rudolf Steiner School in Witten, Germany. Michaela has many publications in German. Her publications in English include *Medicine at the Threshold, A Healing Education, Developmental Insights,* and *A Guide to Child's Health.*

What is Anthroposophic Medicine?

Scientific basis
Therapeutic potential
Prospects for development

Michaela Glöckler

English by Anna R. Meuss

RUDOLF STEINER PRESS

Rudolf Steiner Press
Hillside House, The Square
Forest Row, East Sussex RH18 5ES

www.rudolfsteinerpress.com

Published by Rudolf Steiner Press in 2020

Originally published in German under the title *Was ist Anthroposophische Medizin? Wissenschaftliche Grundlagen, Therapeutische Möglichkeiten, Entwicklungsperspektiven* by Verlag am Goetheanum Dornach, Switzerland, in 2017

A catalogue record for this book is available from the British Library

ISBN 978 1 85584 573 2
Ebook 978 1 85584 511 4

Cover by Andrew Morgan Design
Typeset by Vman InfoTech, Chennai, India
Printed and bound by 4Edge Ltd., Essex

Contents

Publisher's Note

The information in this book is not intended to be taken as a replacement for medical advice. Any person with a condition requiring medical attention should consult a qualified medical practitioner or suitable therapist. The directions for treatment of particular diseases are given for the guidance of medical practitioners only, and should not be prescribed by those who do not have a medical training.

Preface

It is a pleasure to meet the request made by the Verlag am Goetheanum publishers to provide information on anthroposophic medicine. I owe this school of medicine not only vital impulses in my professional work as a paediatrician. As a witness of the times I have also been able to follow the history of this new, integrative approach to medicine for a period of almost 50 years.

At the centre we have the individual with his personal history. Conventional diagnosis and treatment are as much a part of the range of possibilities as the anthroposophic medicines produced by special methods, art therapies, eurythmy therapy and physiotherapy, special needs education, biography work, social therapy and psychotherapy. Added to this are dietary advice, health education and preventive measures as part of an education that promotes health.

But it is the social engagement which fascinates me most with this approach to medicine; it is an inherent part and reflects Rudolf Steiner's call to 'make the health system democratic'.[1] Physicians, pharmacists, manufacturers and consumers are asked, together and in partnership with patients or representatives of civil society, to share responsibility for the development of the health system and to support the multiplicity of methods and the freedom of choice in medicine that will be needed.

An attempt is therefore made in this book to present the spectrum of anthroposophic medicine, including its scientific basis and potential for practice. Added to this are practical examples of its application and tips for external applications when treating patients at home. Suggestions for further reading rounds out the picture.

I am indebted to many people whom I have met professionally. Their trust and readiness to enter into discussion made it possible for me to take part in developing this new approach to treatment.

My thanks to Dagmar Brauer, medical documentarist at the Medical Section at the Goetheanum, for her support and collaboration. Without this it would not have been possible to produce this book.

Michaela Glöckler
Easter 2017
Medical Section at the Goetheanum/Dornach, Switzerland

What Is Anthroposophic Medicine?

Anthroposophic medicine is an integrative system of medicine.[2] Anthroposophic physicians are registered general practitioners and specialists in all fields who combine their scientific training and practice with the study of anthroposophy.[3] Because of this, not only the knowledge and skills of conventional medicine may be used in anthroposophic hospitals but also the therapeutic potential based on insights gained through anthroposophy.[4]

Dutch gynaecologist and general practitioner Ita Wegman, MD (1876–1943), laid the foundations for this new approach to treatment together with Rudolf Steiner, PhD (1861–1925), the founder of anthroposophy.[5,6] She opened a first clinic in Arlesheim/Switzerland in 1921. Further clinics were established in Germany, in Switzerland, Sweden and Italy. Medical practices and treatment centres now exist in more than 90 countries and on all continents.

This development in the twentieth century went parallel with the appearance in the Western world of systems of medicine from the Far East where they evolved in pre-Christian millennia, among them traditional Chinese medicine with pulse diagnosis and acupuncture, different forms of yoga and relaxation techniques, but also methods of Indian, Buddhist ayurvedic medicine (mindfulness techniques, mind-body methods) which are used all over the world today. Anthroposophic medicine and Samuel Hahnemann's (1755–1843) homoeopathy are European contributions in the global endeavour to counterbalance the one-sided aspects of a conventional medicine that takes its orientation from purely natural-scientific paradigms.

How does an anthroposophic physician proceed?

He will only use conventional medication—e.g. fever-reducing antipyretics, anti-inflammatory drugs, antihypertensives to reduce

Ita Wegman (1876–1943)

Rudolf Steiner (1861–1925)

blood pressure, antihistamines to combat allergies, or substitute substances which the body is lacking, sleeping pills that intervene in the biochemical processes in the neural conduction systems as well as psychotropic drugs—where a rapid symptomatic effect is needed. Where this is not absolutely necessary he will carefully check what other regulatory, process-orientated medicines from the anthroposophic or homoeopathic armamentaria, or external applications, eurythmy therapy, art therapy and physical therapy may be indicated. These primarily stimulate self-healing powers and the body's own activities,[7,8,9,10] directly supporting powers of resistance and recovery processes. The example of an influenza epidemic illustrates the usefulness of such process-orientated therapy. With influenza, the virus triggers the symptoms of the disease but does not cause them. If the virus were the cause, almost everyone would develop the disease, for the viruses would be virulent throughout. However, only a small percentage of the population develop influenza. And even if ten per cent of the population were to develop it the question would still be *why nine out of ten did not get influenza*. The answer is simple. People who have a stable immune system, are resistant, would be protected. The body quietly mobilizes its immunological defences so that one does not really notice the viral invasion. Those who do get influenza have to ask themselves why their body's protective functions are failing here and now, and influenza develops with more or less severe signs and symptoms. It is not always easy to find the cause. In the simplest case hypothermia or a cold develops because they are not warmly enough dressed on cold days or are exposed to constant draughts. For viruses multiply best in an organism that has got chilled.[11] On the other hand, weakness due to a prolonged sleep deficit may be responsible or an extended period of inadequate or unhealthy diet, or not enough physical activity. The cause may also be psychological in origin. People who are depressed or tormented by self-doubt, bored, listless, discouraged, anxious or suffer frequent stress are more at risk than those who have positive feelings, a degree of inner calm and 'having got themselves sorted out'. Positive feelings will always stimulate the immune system, negative ones have the opposite effect. The cause may also lie in the sphere of mind and spirit. What does it really depend on for how long one permits oneself negative feelings or lacks in stress tolerance? What must happen so that one comes to a positive identity and attitude to life again, even if circumstances are sad or difficult? It all depends on one's own state of self, on feelings of self-worth and the way in which one establishes one's identity. Those who can see their life, their destiny—with all the highs and lows—as their personal development will find motives for what might be learned or done right now in any given situation. Resilience studies have provided most valuable proof of the high degree to which the way one handles oneself and the chosen lifestyle influence health in body and soul.[12]

Works like Viktor Frankl's *Man's Search for Meaning*, Jacques Lusseyran's *And there was Light*, or Hans Jonas' *Mortality and Morality, Search for Good After Auschwitz* are moving examples. These people survived in spite of all the inhumanity they had to suffer or observe. What kept them alive was the growing certainty of their lasting existence and destiny in spirit. A few months before his death the Protestant theologian Dietrich Bonhoeffer was able to write the following prayer which is now well known to all confessions, its power and might touching one deeply even when just reading it:

> Kind spirits lovingly around us
> We fearlessly await what is to come;
> God be with us at night and in the morning
> And most assuredly on every new day.[13]

Countless stories of what happened to refugees in our day also speak of the great powers (of endurance) given by trust in God, in oneself and in destiny. They made it possible to survive extreme difficulties. The will to survive and hope of a better life will then be so dominant that the immune system will resist and bear whatever comes, be it exhaustion, heat, cold, lack of food and water, fear and violence.

So how should one treat an attack of influenza, especially if one cannot really identify the causes since they are not yet evident to the sick person or he does not want to talk about them? In every case it is a good idea to take the message of the illness seriously and arrange for a time of recovery and reflection. On the other hand it is not a good idea to try and suppress the symptoms as far and fast as possible with medicines to reduce the temperature and relieve pain, and then live on exactly as before. This would only be indicated if something important absolutely had to be done first or was at risk, so that one could not think of time for rest and recuperation until later on. In any case, it is important to support the development of the necessary new balanced state of health. This requires medicines capable of achieving it, with process-orientated action that did not merely deal with symptoms.

The above-mentioned five categories of causes for sickness and of healing were also listed by Paracelsus (1493–1541) who called them *quinque entibus*, five instances.[14,15] Sickness and healing thus occur in five different ways:

1) Physically due to influences from outside.
2) In the sphere of self-regulation and vital processes.

3) At the level of inner experience.
4) In the sphere of the I's inherent influences.
5) Due to the way in which we think and feel about ourselves, the world and other people, and our philosophy of life or spiritual orientation according to which we configure our life.

Why Have Anthropsophy In Medicine?

Anthroposophy (*anthropos* = human being, *Sophia* = wisdom, knowledge) is still considered to be difficult to understand. People know of many anthroposophic initiatives in special education and education, agriculture and medicine, but the integrative image of world and man which is the anthroposophy behind it, tends to be rather vague. One is not really sure if it is a philosophy, a kind of religion or a difficult, or even eclectic philosophy of life. As the anthroposophic institutions and initiatives are often quite successful, people will also ask if it really needs this anthroposophic superstructure and if one could not do something equally good without it.

Why the need for anthroposophy? What reason can there be to be interested in it?

There are four aspects to anthroposophy and all four of them may arouse interest and lead to further enquiries or only the one or the other aspect may do so.

The philosophical aspect

The philosophical basis of anthroposophy is a further development of Goethe's approach to science and of German idealism with its ideals of freedom and dignity, truth and love.[16,17,18] Philosophy is not important to some people—one would like to have good ideas for work and life and not waste time on intellectual brooding. But there are others who become anthroposophists only because here they find an epistemology, a theory of knowledge, and its philosophical background that help them to gain better insight into themselves and their relationship to the world. Professor Peter Heusser, head of the Department of Theory of Medicine, Integrative and Anthroposophic Medicine at Witten-Herdecke University, in his habitation dissertation established that epistemology was the basis of anthroposophic medicine. Rudolf Steiner worked for many years at the Goethe-Schiller Archives in Weimar to edit Goethe's scientific works, entering deeply into Goethe's holistic way of gaining insight in practical life. With the greatest possible appreciation he later named his school of anthroposophy in Dornach, Switzerland, the Goetheanum.[19]

Philosophy is the art of independent thinking. In his main work, *The Philosophy of Spiritual Activity* [alternative title: *The Philosophy of Freedom*] Steiner formulated this art of insight challenge as follows: 'One must face up to the idea in living experience; otherwise it will hold one in bondage.'[20] That is, if you accept the thoughts and ideas of others and do not think them through and evaluate them yourself, you will be dependent on the authorities from whom the thoughts have come. With the help of this approach—see for yourself, question, consider, understand—all students of anthroposophy are encouraged to reflect *their own philosophy*.

The aspect of taking charge of one's own development

Anthroposophy involves a way of individual training which leads to further development of the psyche, the gaining of self-knowledge, and a strengthening of the will.[21] Today many people are searching for an inter-religious way of spiritual self experience. They do not wish to join a particular confession or specific spiritual grouping. They are looking for a generally human way of inner development. Some of them find this in anthroposophy and its organizations.[22] The Anthroposophical Society is organized internationally and open to all scientific, religious and artistic convictions and so one finds here representatives of many different spiritual orientations. People of the Christian confessions, of Buddhism, Daoism, Shintoism, the Hindi religion, of Zarathustra spirituality, Judaism and some representatives of Islam, as well as many who have no specific spiritual orientation, can here learn more about their own spiritual identity by also taking up the individual inner training of anthroposophy. What unites them in this society is the concept of development in anthroposophy and the endeavour to make social and cultural life more human and fruitful for the future. In a paper which has attracted widespread attention among natural scientists, the biologist Bernd Rosslenbroich has shown that the autonomy principle is inherent in the whole of evolution, culminating in human evolution.[23] This autonomy principle is also the basis for individual inner training. It is not easy to grow aware of this and live it constructively. Failure and starting over and over again are part of it, just as quietly giving one's own life the necessary direction and working on the ideals of true humanity: truthfulness, love, freedom and dignity.

The aspect of spiritual science

Anthroposophy is available in the form of the collected works of Rudolf Steiner. He has presented a rich abundance of spiritual facts, content and wisdom in fundamental books and articles and about 6,000[24] lectures given to specialists and lay people. To the superficial view some of it may appear like a collection of the knowledge already established in the theosophical and mystic Christian tradition or elements which Steiner investigated with reference to many great minds in the history of civilization, with genius bringing them together in wider contexts. Taking a closer look one does, however, perceive the authenticity and personal signature of Steiner, something even his critics cannot deny.[25] Peter Sloterdijk did therefore call him 'a perfectly normal genius'.[26]

Considering that it was suggested that he had scraped his knowledge together and not obtained it in an authentic way, Steiner himself said in a lecture to members of the medical profession: 'I must not forget to make you aware that what I am saying here is not taken from earlier medical works but is fully based on present-day spiritual-scientific investigations. However, one must try every now and then and go back to the earlier literature for the terminology, for the more recent literature has not yet developed a terminology in this direction. But someone who would think that something which is said here has simply been taken from earlier literature would be very much mistaken.'[27] The perceptions of man and world, nature and spirit presented by him are, as he said, the result of his own investigations using the spiritual science of his day which is therefore referred to as anthroposophic *science of the spirit*. Initially he would also follow ancient spiritual tradition and speak of 'occult science'.[28]

The complex abundance of spiritual facts which Rudolf Steiner presented to his audiences has led to anthroposophy being considered close to philosophy and religion. He did however emphasize again and again that the descriptions he gave and the points of view taken were knowledge he had gained by his own efforts and were presented as knowledge or insights and not matters of belief. People were asked to take what he said as stimulating ideas, as working hypothesis, and test for themselves if they will stand up to their own experiences in life and their search for insight, and if they can serve life. He also hoped that readers with an academic background would make the effort to substantiate his insights, gained by the path of meditation, with the aid of empirical studies.[29] Steiner was thus putting the emphasis in scientific discussions on the principle of *internal or inner evidence*. Anything one has perceived to be right—based on experience and insight—one feels to be 'inwardly evident'. It does then also require external evidence before one can, with the help of reproducible facts, show that the matter one has perceived to be right is indeed legitimate. It needs the two kinds of evidence to establish a comprehensive insight and the possibility to arrive at a view of man and the world which can do justice to spiritual and material requirements.

In how far is anthroposophic medicine therefore an 'ideological medicine'?

In all fairness every form of medicine reflects a particular view of man, nature and environment. Natural-scientific materialism is also an ideology, as are idealism, realism and other philosophical or spiritual approaches. Anyone who thinks that he does not have a philosophy of life has not yet reflected on his own standpoint and what supports it. This lack of reflection is one of the main obstacles to giving recognition to the normality of anthroposophic medicine. A philosophy that has been individually arrived at must be clearly distinguished from philosophical associations or communities of faith that take their orientation from authorities.

It is because anthroposophy is based on individuals developing autonomy that one does, especially among anthroposophists, find marked pluralism of opinions and standpoints, even the frequently quoted 'culture of strife'. The history of the Anthroposophical Society is full of notable crises and conflicts that tell of the struggle for individual and social competence, a struggle that is far from easy. It is all the more good to know that to this day the society has not split into different groupings but the will to understand one another and develop tolerance of those who think differently has always gained the upper hand.

The poet and anthroposophist Christian Morgenstern (1871–1914) wrote a poem which is a masterpiece in showing this tension between the necessary individualization on the one hand and the ability to create community on the other:

Seeking the truth
You are on your own;
No one can walk
By your side.
For a bit we do walk,
It seems, side by side,
But in the end we know
That everyone has gone.
Even the most beloved
Struggles far away;
But in achieving the goal
You win through to a star,
Making new ground for God

Wholly Christian now—
Brothers and sisters
For evermore.[30]

Here a true artist has shown that the greatest possible individualism and community in the spirit do not have to be in opposition. In fact, the ideals of the French Revolution—the freedom of the individual, equality and fraternal solidarity—can only thus be seen in their true light. If one knows that everyone has to follow his own path, respect for the uniqueness and dignity of others will grow, and we do, at the same time, find that this factual situation makes us equal. Since we are both equal and individually very different we do again and again have to depend on the help of our brothers and sisters. This will be effective if one is able to see the needs of the other, respect and as far as possible meet them.

But what is 'spirit' as the foundation of this anthroposophic and spiritual-scientific view of the world?
The answer is simple: human thought.

Normally we all know the state of having thoughts, knowing, informing oneself or moving in recognized or pre-established patterns of thought and being able to express them. However, starting from one's *own* thinking activity one also discovers *the one who is thinking* in his thinking. Johann Gottlieb Fichte, idealist philosopher, would again and again draw his students' attention to the central importance of this spiritual self experience in thinking. He took them through the following exercise:

He would ask them if they could see the wall of the lecture theatre. He would then say, 'Close your eyes and think the wall.'

And then came the decisive request, 'And now think the one who has been thinking the wall ...'

Doing this one can experience how in one's thinking one's own self comes to awareness as pure source spring of activity, as inner readiness to be active, as I, as using one's own will, purely energetic, spiritual experience of self, as it were.[31] Starting from direct experience of self or I in this way in his powers of thought, the individual will have gained the certain starting point for developing his own view of the world.[32,33] He may be said to have found his own feet in mind and spirit and is able to develop wider and wider perspectives in his thinking. The more he understands, the more he 'sees' of the world. And the more the world interests him and invites reflection, the more differentiated and clear will his thinking be. To understand oneself and the world and thus arrive at an authentic view of self and world—that may be said to be the philosophy of anthroposophy. To show one's contemporaries that with thinking they may come to the reality of the spirit—that was one of Rudolf Steiner's central concerns. To gain living experience of one's own I by thinking, experiencing it as a spiritual reality, will at the same time reveal the spiritual dimension of human dignity as autonomous competence in awareness of the spirit.[34,35,36,37] Towards the end of his life Rudolf Steiner did once more put it like this: *Anthroposophy is a way of gaining insight by which one seeks to take man's spiritual nature to the spiritual element in the universe.*[38] The thinking done by every individual forms the basis for this. Hannah Arendt called this experience of self 'thinking without the handrail'.[39]

The anthropological aspect and the image of man

John Scotus Eriugena

In anthroposophy the image of man is, on the one hand, based on the tradition of the occident in cultural history, and on the other hand on autonomous practice of gaining insight that we referred to in the last chapter. In the early Middle Ages the monk John Scotus Eriugena (815–877) considered the question as to how man relates to nature in dialogue form in his work *The*

Division of Nature.[40] This relates directly to the anthroposophic study of man and nature. He wrote:

> *What does man have in common with the mineral world?*
> *The answer was: the solid body.*
> *And what does he have in common with the plants?*
> *The answer: life.*
> *And what does man have in common with the animals?*
> *The answer: the soul.*
> *And then the fourth question: And what does man have in common with the world of angels?*
> *The answer: thinking.*
> *Then comes the last, decisive question:*
> *And what does man have entirely on his own—in common only with himself and his own kind?*
> *The answer: independent judgement.*

The German word for 'judgement' or 'personal opinion' is *Urteil.* The first syllable, *Ur-*, means 'origin, beginning'. The second syllable, *—teil,* is something which only has meaning with reference to the whole, the original. The verb *urteilen* is to make the part relate meaningfully to the whole. In anthroposophic anthropology the focus is on this integrative, anthropocentric approach. Everything people have around them—including the lawful nature of the cosmos and the starry heavens—relates to them in a specific way, and this needs to be assessed and understood.

Christian Morgenstern wrote of this aspect of wholeness, with every individual able to see and experience himself when making a judgement. He gave this poem the title 'The washing of the feet'.[41] It shows in particular how one natural world serves the other and they are all related and dependent on one another.

> *The washing of the feet*
>
> Thank you, silent stone,
> I bow down before you:
> I owe to you my plant existence.
> I thank you, soil and plants,

Bowing down before you.
You helped me rise to animal nature.
I thank you, stone, herb and animal,
Bowing down before you:
Together the three of you made me who I am.

We thank you, human being,
And come before you in harmony;
For it is because you are that we are.
Thanks arise from all divine oneness
And all divine manifoldness.
All that is does join in saying thanks.

The mineral, plant, animal and human worlds around us take individual form in the human being, his own, complex fourfold constitution—body, life, soul and spirit. This fourfold constitution is called physical, etheric, astral and I organization in anthroposophic anthropology.

Physical organization. Laws of the solid state of aggregation of matter, mineral and spatial nature of man.

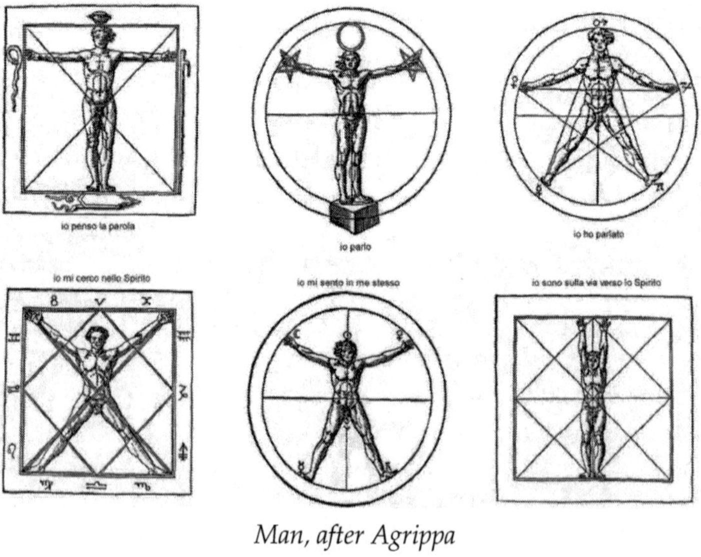

Man, after Agrippa

Etheric organization (αιθήρ). Laws of the fluid state of aggregation of matter as the basis for all life.

Ether is the Greek term for the blue sky filled with sunlight. Plants owe to it the development of chlorophyll, the vehicle for their energy. Life would not be possible on earth if there were no sunlight or biorhythms. Life progresses in time and is regulated by rhythms arising through the movements of the heavenly bodies—planets, sun and earth. Hence the words of Paracelsus: 'Eating a plant you eat the universe.'[42]

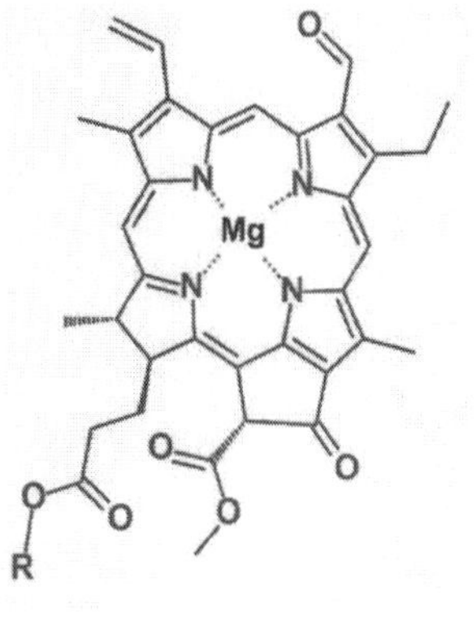

Chlorophyll molecule

Photosynthesis in leaf

Astral organization. Laws of the airy and gaseous state of aggregation as the basis of our breathing, speech, movement and expression of inner feelings.

The word *aster* comes from Latin and means 'star'. Not only life, but the soul, too, has its origin in the cosmos and senses its heavenly home in the laws that govern the world of stars. The differentiated world of stars is also a kind of archetype of the wide variety of human relationship constellations—quite apart from the familiar astrological traditions and relationships with human nature. We love 'sun, moon and stars' like something related to us, and in poetry and literature it is not only they but also the wind, the weather, times of the day and the year which are used as metaphors to give expression to particular feelings and inner moods.

I organization. Laws governing heat and thermodynamics as the basis for the 'I' experience. This is always warm. In Genesis we read 'God created man in his image'. In experiencing temperatures we feel related to everything to which our hearts

Earth as a star, seen from the universe

may warm, be it physical or non-physical. And so the I organization also lives in the laws of warmth or heat, not substantially, not a state of aggregation, although they do govern the existence of matter. The body temperature may be just two degrees more or less and metabolic function and well-being will be seriously affected, as are whole eco systems as evident in global warming. Warmth or heat has extensive and intensive effects. It can thus be the bridge from inner warmth in soul and spirit to physical body temperature. This oneness experienced with warmth or heat can therefore also be the basis for coherent spiritual and physical experience of the I or self.

In his *Occult Science*[43] Rudolf Steiner has given a detailed description of the evolution of this fourfold human constitution, relating it to the natural laws of the states of aggregation and of heat. He was also consistent in saying that something which is spiritual by nature exists in relation to all material things.

Basing himself on the terminology of the Christian system of hierarchies and angels of Dionysius the Areopagite he wrote of the relationship between the evolving human being and this world of divine spirits. At the centre of it all is the Mystery on Golgotha, i.e. the life and death of the Christ on earth and for humankind: 'Rightly understood, the Christ impulse enables the human soul which has taken it in to feel itself to be part of a spiritual world, recognizing this and acting accordingly, having previously been outside that world. ... Thus the seed of love is planted in the inmost core of essential human nature. And from there it is to flow into the whole of evolution.'[44]

These complex concepts of the four levels of human existence have today also been affirmed by studies in systems science. Higher, interlinked form-givers and process configurers have been discovered or adopted as hypotheses. These are labelled with field concepts or taken intra-organically, like the ordering of mathematical and geometric symmetry and asymmetry which cannot be explained by Darwin's paradigms of selection, mutation and adaptation.[45,46]

The question of symmetry as a universal causal principle is also part of this. Ultimately it is thoughts, laws, wider regulatory situations which are reflected in the arrangement and transformations of evolution or take them forward. It is merely

Caspar David Friedrich: Cross in the Mountains *(Tetschen Altar, 1808)*

important to think of these regulatory elements as effective 'energies' or power systems. Thoughts and laws are something real if non-physical, and not 'nothing'.

Interesting in this context are the concepts of auto-regulation, self-regulation or self-healing which are, at present, widely used in conventional medicine. A differentiated view is taken of them in diagnosis and treatment in anthroposophic medicine, depending on how much the levels of existence, i.e. the physical, etheric and astral organizations and the I are involved in self-regulation in a given case. They serve diagnosis and treatment as the regulative principles for interpreting signs and symptoms, laboratory findings or imaging methods such as X-ray, ultrasound, magnetic resonance tomography/MRT, etc. in a way that is in accord with the essential nature and the resulting approach to treatment. It is thus possible to develop a holistic view of the individual based on physical condition, vitality and evidence of the mental and spiritual condition.[47,48]

Understanding Health and Sickness

To get an integrative concept of health and sickness one needs above all to have a good idea of how processes work. Where do we find this? Which view of the human being is simple enough to meet the needs of daily practice and yet also sufficiently complex to integrate the multiple aspects of human nature, including the steadily growing abundance of scientific facts and uncommon symptoms?

The questions may seem elementary, but they are not easy to answer. How does sickness actually develop? How does it vanish again? How can health be regained again and again in the ups and downs of life, in growth and development, in crisis and ageing? Where does decompensation have its boundary if today you were still just in health and the next day are clearly aware that you are no longer in good shape? Under what conditions are processes encouraged that will ultimately produce the symptoms and can no longer be regulated by the organism's self-healing powers? How can such morbid processes be reversed? Every system of medicine can provide further understanding. In anthroposophic diagnosis and treatment the concept of four levels of existence brings new insights. For laws are described here that can be the bridge between physiological, bodily processes and those in soul and spirit, i.e. purely mental. Take the complexity and multiformity of possible causes of disease and their overcoming into account. (See also p. 24ff.)

Physiological way of thinking and method of treatment

The basic ethics of anthroposophic physicians and their diagnostic and therapeutic assessment of the morbid situation are determined by the way they see the human being. The idea of the laws pertaining to four levels of existence interactive in developing and maturing the bodily and mental constitution also leads to a way of thinking with physiological process orientation. It enables one to form an opinion that does justice to the situation even where results of scientific trials are not yet available or, where they do exist, to make a critical assessment of them if required.

Three examples from paediatrics will illustrate this. In that field it is particularly important to monitor processes of development and maturing. Diseases will here often reflect physical and/or mental problems with adaptation to the challenges coming from outside. Or they are the result of the incarnating individual nature in the child's increasing struggle with the physical organization 'inherited' from the parents. In childhood it is therefore important to treat an acute disease in a process-orientated rather than symptom-orientated way. Steiner did already use a genome concept that considered the genotype to be capable of learning and developing, something well substantiated in epigenetic science in recent decades. He also recommended sensitive handling of febrile infections and childhood diseases, for these can effect a positive regulation of the genotype, making it possible for the incarnating child to adapt the inherited physical organization better to his own needs and his will to express himself.[49,50,51]

It was and is typical for anthroposophic physicians to be cautious in the use of antipyretics and antibiotics. For a temperature is a natural reaction of the body to accelerate processes of adaptation and change or to help them to win through. The immunostimulant effect of a temperature and its potential influence on the genotype's mode of function is generally known today. It was taken into account even before anthroposophic medicine began, thanks to the holistic image of man with the I organization and a concept of heredity that included potential for development. Instead of antipyretics it was suggested to use external applications and regulatory medicines in homoeopathic preparations to support the body's own defences even if the disease would take slightly longer than with conventional treatment. Recovery would be stable as a rule, with little danger of relapse. At the back of the family medicine chest there would, however, be antipyretic suppositories for the (rare) cases when the body's self-regulation did not adequately deal with the temperature.

It was not until the second half of the twentieth century that this method was also scientifically substantiated by research done in conventional medicine. Immunological investigations showed that a temperature is not a disease nor a symptom to be removed as quickly as possible. Instead, pyrexia was seen to be meaningful as part of the body's defences. It was found that the multiplication of viruses and bacteria is impeded at an optimum temperature of 39 to 41 °C and a temperature is the best way of destroying them.[52]

Yet when it comes to caution in the use of antibiotics, it was not until the beginning of the 1990s that this was also recommended in conventional medicine. Studies were then published which showed that even otitis media (inner ear infection) does not always require antibiotics—strictly required in conventional medicine until then—that is, by routine exhibition—to treat every infection. This is no longer permitted. One reason for this is also the serious problem of resistance to antibiotics following excessive use of these drugs for humans and widespread abuse in animal husbandry. It would be desirable to add the alternative ways of treating febrile infections in hospitals and medical centres. They have already become well established in many places in domestic nursing and self-medication.[53] In one of the October issues in 2016 it says on the title page of the weekly magazine *Focus*: 'Grandma was right after all.' Typical home remedies based on long tradition were pictured under that headline.

Like their colleagues in homoeopathy and complementary medicine, anthroposophic physicians do not use antipyretics and antibiotics routinely but they are carefully considered in the individual case. They have thus for a long time made a contribution which it is worth following in counteracting the widely discussed resistance to antibiotics.[54]

The third example concerns the use of vitamin D_3 in the prevention and treatment of rickets in infants and young children. The first anthroposophic paediatrician, Wilhelm zur Linden (1896–1972) and anthroposophic GPs found their own way of working with the vitamin D substitution treatment originally recommended by medical scientists. They recommended small physiological doses. They invested a great deal of time in consultations so that parents would, as far as possible, enable their infants to develop vitamin D_3 naturally, in sunlight.[55,56,57] In conventional medicine the recommendation to give small doses and proceed in a process-orientated way only came when the damage due to high doses had become evident.[58]

These examples may show that a holistic approach like that used in anthroposophy does not necessarily have to be unscientific. On the contrary, it can bring scientific findings closer to real life and on occasion even foresee them. In any case, the undesirable side effects which are inevitable if thinking is reductionist and not enough attention is paid to the regulative context can be avoided or at least limited.

The four levels of human existence and Aristotle's Categories

Our knowledge of body, soul and spirit is as old as humanity itself. Reference to it does not make anthroposophy and its approach to medicine original. As mentioned above, Steiner's contribution has been a new way of entering into these four fields of experience. In the terminology he used in medicine and education he employed the terms 'body' or 'organization',[59] as already mentioned. These not only define the relationship between the natural worlds and the states of aggregation but also stand for the differentiated whole of human nature in spirit (I organization), soul (astral organization), life (etheric organization) and body (physical organization). They show that these are complex combinations of laws through which human beings can perceive, experience, express themselves and be active:

— as a solid form in space,
— as living creatures between birth and death in a developmental process in time,
— as a soul with entirely personal sentience and
— as a spirit gifted with autonomy.

Aristotle knew and described these levels of human existence in his theory of the four elements. But in his theory of categories he also asked questions which clearly bring out the qualities of the categories and how they become evident. They also cast light on the anthroposophic system of four levels of existence.

For the *physical organization* those are the categories of space:

Location: *ubi*, πoυ (pou)
Position: *situs*, κεισθαι (keisthai)
Quantity in amount and size: *quantitas*, ποσον (poson)
Having possession: *habitus*, εχειν (echein)

The *etheric organization* includes the categories:

Time: when, quando, ποτε (poté)
Quality: *qualitas*, ποιον (poion)
Relation: relationship, *relation*, προς τι (pros ti)

The *astral organization* includes:

Action, doing: *actio*, ποιειν (poiein)
Passion, undergoing: *passio*, πασχειν (paschein)

The I organization is determined by the Substance/Essence category, called ουσια. This term has the complex meaning of 'existence' and 'essential nature', thus both spiritual and physical, material substance. In Latin *ousia* is *sub-stantia*, meaning something located underneath (sub). In Greek it could still be thought and formulated as spiritual and physical entity of spirit and matter. In Latin usage it did become more differentiated into something more on the purely material side.

In anthroposophic medicine one therefore puts specific questions:

- What must be done 'at the site' of the changes, using a local, symptom-related method?
- Which vital processes need to be supported, with what qualities?
- How can art therapy or biography studies initiate processes of harmonizing the soul which will then act on the body, establishing order?
- How can a person's identity, the substance of his essential nature, be strengthened so that one can also contribute whatever is possible for oneself to aid recovery? (See pp. 47ff. and 51ff.)

This system of levels of existence or the expression of human nature also exists in the ayurvedic tradition and in the concepts of energy flow and streams in other traditional forms of medicine that are based on a spiritual view of the human being.

Hermann Schmitz, professor of philosophy at Kiel University until 1993, was at that time developing a phenomenological concept, working out these levels of human nature for clinical observation.[60] Today the number of therapies based on level theories continues to increase, for instance also the well-known biopsychosocial model.[61]

Something new added by the anthroposophic medical approach is total integration of the conventional medical science and way of thinking. This does not only open up a satisfying prospect of individual self-perception as a human being but also permits a new, complex theory concerning the questions as to how sickness develops and how healing processes can be understood.[62] (See p. 3ff.)

The connection between body and soul

In 1917 Rudolf Steiner published the results of 30 years of investigations into the connection between body and soul in the appendix to his book, *Von Seelenrätseln*[63] (Riddles of the Soul).

He had come to the conclusion that the capacities of the human soul are not produced by the nervous system but that they develop and use that system. What is more, he realized that the basic capacities of the soul—thinking, feeling and acting out

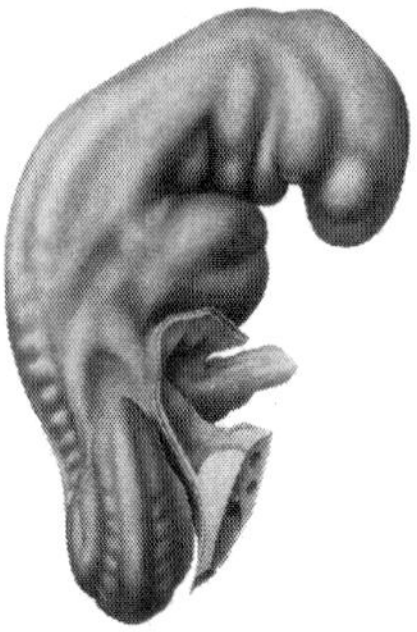

Embryo at the end of the 1st month (size: 3.4 mm)

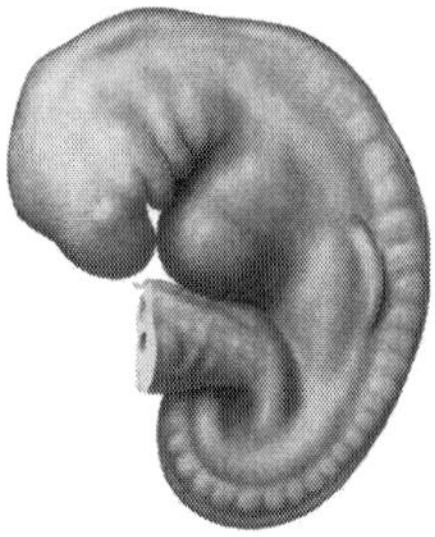

Embryo at the end of the 2nd month (size: 4.2 mm)

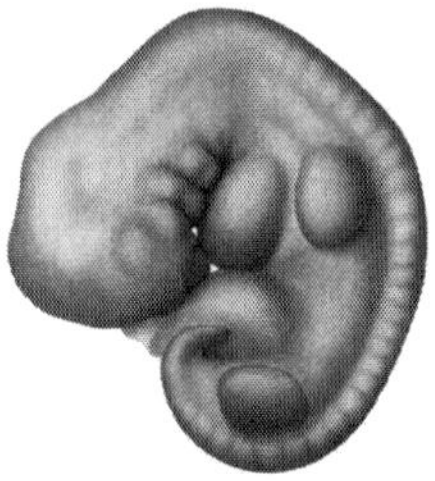

Embryo at about 5 weeks (size: 6.3 mm)

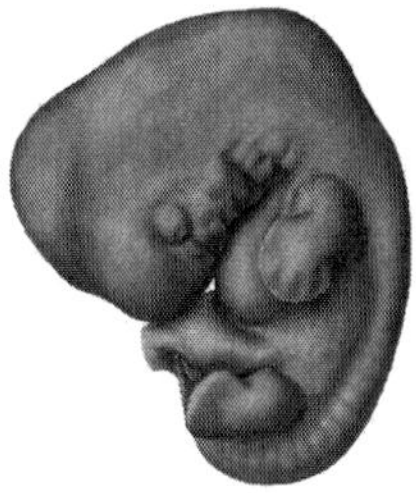

Embryo at about 6 weeks (size: 10 mm)

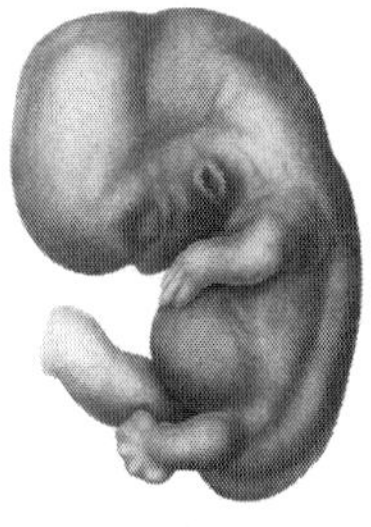

Embryo at the end of the 2nd month (size: 17.5 mm)

of the will—reflect the *whole* human being. This whole human being does, however, have a specific threefold configuration, and this, from the third or fourth week of embryonic development onwards, is evident in the stages of embryonic development[64] depicted on page 27.

Steiner discovered that only thinking in full conscious awareness and sensory observation rest on the functions of the neurosensory system—including the ideas we are able to develop of our experiences in feeling and will. On the other hand he found the life of feeling to be in direct functional resonance with the functional rhythms of the cardiovascular system and respiration. Activity based on the will he considered to reflect the activity of metabolism and limbs.

'One just has to see the physiology of the breathing rhythm in the right light and one will comprehensively come to accept the words "the soul has living experience in feeling by using the support of the breathing rhythm much as it uses that of the physiology of the nerves when forming ideas." And when it comes to acting out of the will, one finds that this does in a similar way use the support of metabolic processes. Once again one has to consider the many branches and projections of the metabolic processes in the whole organism. How, when something is envisaged, a process occurs in the nerves that makes the soul conscious of what it envisages and furthermore when something is "felt", a modification of the breathing rhythm makes a feeling come alive in the soul, and when something is to be done, a metabolic process occurs which is the bodily basis for the soul's experience of acting out of the will.'[65]

Professor Johannes Rohen at Erlangen University took account of this functional threefold anatomical order in his anatomy textbooks. Professor Wolfgang Schad applied this aspect in a consistent presentation of the development of vertebrate animals compared to human beings.[66] Steiner was aware that his discovery of threefold soul function in conjunction with the scientific background to the threefold system of body and physiology would require a major, comprehensive publication and this he was unable to produce during the First World War.

He wrote: 'It is perfectly possible to establish the reasons using the existing scientific means. That would be the subject of a major publication which the present situation does not permit me to write.'[67] Schad and Rohen have since been able to do this work to an appreciable degree.

The paradigm of body-creating levels of existence and those that are active free of the body

At the very heart of anthroposophic medicine is the effort to connect conventional medical and scientific thinking with the identity of man in soul and spirit and his self-knowledge. The new paradigm which does make this possible in real terms is the law of metamorphosis discovered by Rudolf Steiner, the metamorphosis of the function of the levels of human existence in creating the body into an activity that is purely spiritual, taking effect out of the body. How can we think and understand this? Rudolf Steiner's discovery was that the levels of human existence are purely spiritual regulative laws (see page 21) that take effect and come to expression not only in the body's growth and development. To the degree to which growth has been achieved, they will also appear out of body, as it were, in a state of purely immaterial activities in soul and spirit that cannot be perceived through the senses. Rudolf Steiner did here speak of a genuine metamorphosis of body-related activity of the levels of existence into an out-of-body activity in soul and spirit as evident in the figure on the next page. This shows how this metamorphosis happens in the course of life, culminating in death, when the physical organization is completely abandoned by level-of-existence activity, that is, by etheric, astral and I organization. Only the physical, mineral organism and its laws remain at death, and the body will then also decompose according to those laws. The etheric, astral and I organizations, on the other hand, enter into their post-mortem existence and this is the precondition for individual life after death, with experiences gained on earth worked through, and preparations made for a next stage of development on earth.

- — The part of the etheric organization that gives life to the physical appears out of body as *eternal life* in thought.
- — Astral organization bringing sensitive inwardness and awareness to the enlivened physical organization, differentiating it right down to its smallest cell structures, appears out of body as differentiated world of feelings.
- — The I organization which makes the human constitution the vehicle for the individual spirit appears out of body as 'free will' that experiences itself as not to be dependent on the energy and functional state of the body.

Friedrich Schiller, physician and poet, saw this situation in philosophical terms and wrote of it in his letters, *On the Aesthetic Education of Man*.[68] In his *Wallenstein* play he let the protagonist say: 'It is the spirit which builds the body for itself!.'[69]

The figure below may serve to illustrate this.

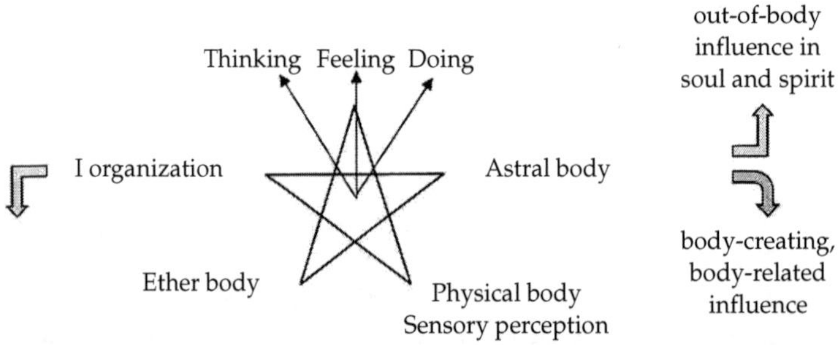

Body-related and out-of-body influences of the levels of human existence

This is clearly evident in embryonic development. Three processes of central significance apply throughout:

1) Proliferation, i.e. cell growth.
2) Differentiation, i.e. all tissues derive from one (stem) cell type and differentiate into the different tissues.

3) Integration, i.e. growth and differentiation, must be well attuned to one another as they proceed so that configuration may be harmonious.

In anthroposophic interpretation the etheric organization gives impulses for growth, the astral organization those for differentiation and the I organization those for integration.

How do thinking, feeling and doing (acting out of the will) differ when it comes to direct experience?

- Thinking shows itself to be 'creative', generating, configuring and reconfiguring—like a sculptor.
- Feeling is experienced like inner music—mood, differentiating interval, tone and resonance, dissonance and harmony.
- Acting out of the will conveys the experience of identity, concentration, reflection of energy and consistency.

The levels of human existence also interact with one another, as shown by Rudolf Steiner speaking of 'body' rather than 'organization'.[70]

The I body gives	form	in the physical
	inner movement	in the etheric
	inner life	in the astral
	soul quality	in the spiritual
The astral body gives	movement	in the physical
	desire	in the etheric
	feeling	in the astral
	thinking	in the spiritual
The ether body gives	experience of self	in the physical
	self-knowledge	in the etheric
	feeling	in the astral
	thinking	in the spiritual
The physical body gives	egoity = *inwardness*	in the physical
	idea	in the etheric
	sentience, feeling	in the astral
	perception	in the spiritual

Spiritual orientation

The way of thinking (ether body, out of the body) , feeling (astral body, out of the body) and acting out of the will (doing, I organization, out of the body) serves to develop soul and spirit and has a beneficial or disruptive effect on the system of the levels of human existence.

I organization provides for physical and spiritual experience of identity; out of the body it functions to act out of the will

Astral body provides for development of conscious awareness on the border between inside and outside, experience of inner space possible; out of the body it functions as empathy and emotional activity

Ether body provides for processes of development and self-healing; out of the body it functions as activity out of the will

Physical body provides for individualization, 'experience of egoity'; perception of the world through the senses with the aid of the sense organs and their particular relationship with light, sound, colours and other qualities in the surrounding world

The four levels of human existence in their significance for the development of basic mental and spiritual activities and their effect on physiology

The sketch cannot be considered in more detail in this brief publication. It would need a separate publication on the way in which the levels of existence interact. The sketch does, however, encourage reflection and self-observation and we do therefore reproduce it here. The figure sums up the activities of the levels of existence in a simplified form in terms of physical effects and influences on soul and spirit.

Laws governing embryonic development and the efficacy of art therapies

One particular characteristic of embryonic development is its holistic nature and synchronicity. Yet how is this process conducted? In spite of all efforts made, no central 'regulator gene' has so far been found. In fact, the genetic information elements of a particular organ such as the eye do not lie close together, as one might have thought, but are distributed among different chromosomes. As with a symphony orchestra, where instruments located in various places on stage must sound together to create music, that is how configuration comes about. In view of this fact Steiner took a firm stand—as shown above—referring to the I organization and its laws as the artist who calls on the other bodies representing the levels of human existence to work together in harmony:

— the physical body with its spatial and architectural functionality;
— the ether body with its proliferative, creative activity, analogous to a sculptor;
— the astral body with its differentiating and polarizing laws, the equivalent of a musician;
— the I organization, on the other hand, like a speech artist who can convey the sculptural quality of consonants and the vowel quality in speech, integrating all the laws.

Some impressive research findings have at any rate shown that art therapies do not only stimulate the creative abilities of the soul but also regenerate the whole bodily constitution, bringing order into it (see chapter on art therapies).

The development of thinking in accord with the physical maturing and ageing of the organism

The figure which follows on p. 35 shows on the left side the human body's most important anatomical and physiological stages of maturation, parallel to the development of thinking, and on the right side the stages of involution and ageing.

From birth until about the ninth year of life it is the development of the nervous system and the sense organs which predominates. Then come the organs of the rhythmic functional order. Their maturation—including harmonization of breathing and cardiac rhythm frequencies—concludes only by the fifteenth or sixteenth year. Full maturation of the skeletal system of the adult form, stabilization of the metabolic processes and hormonal system takes longest to achieve. It is not complete until about the twentieth to twenty-third year.

Steiner's concept of the metamorphosis which the levels of existence go through from body-related to body-free activity in soul and spirit is substantiated when one compares these phases of bodily maturation with the corresponding age-typical thought patterns. Up to the ninth year thinking is primarily determined by the functional dynamics coming free as the growth processes reach completion. The forming of accurate ideas and the ability to remember grow progressively more precise and true to sensory perceptions. Puberty, on the other hand, sees the culmination of a thinking activity that does not provide for new or even better powers of memory and development of ideas, but does, rather, concern the way in which one handles one's ideas. The functional dynamics of dialectical thinking emerge, a thinking where one is able to think the opposite of what someone else is putting forward at the given moment. Thinking in opposites, coming alive through contradiction—this is typical for thinking in puberty. That is the period of development when the cardiovascular system and the respiratory organs mature, their functions determined by the opposition principle.

From the 15th year onwards the typically idealistic thinking of youth and early adulthood develops. One learns to stand on one's own feet in one's thinking, establish an appropriate standpoint, and feel enthusiasm for ideas. This correlates with the maturing of the metabolic organs and the system of limbs as they release their powers of growth and make them available for thinking activities. One is aflame for something, able to vouch for something and take full responsibility. Independent thought indicates emancipation of powers of growth from the skeletal system, whereas we owe spiritual warmth and creativity to the maturing of the metabolic organs.

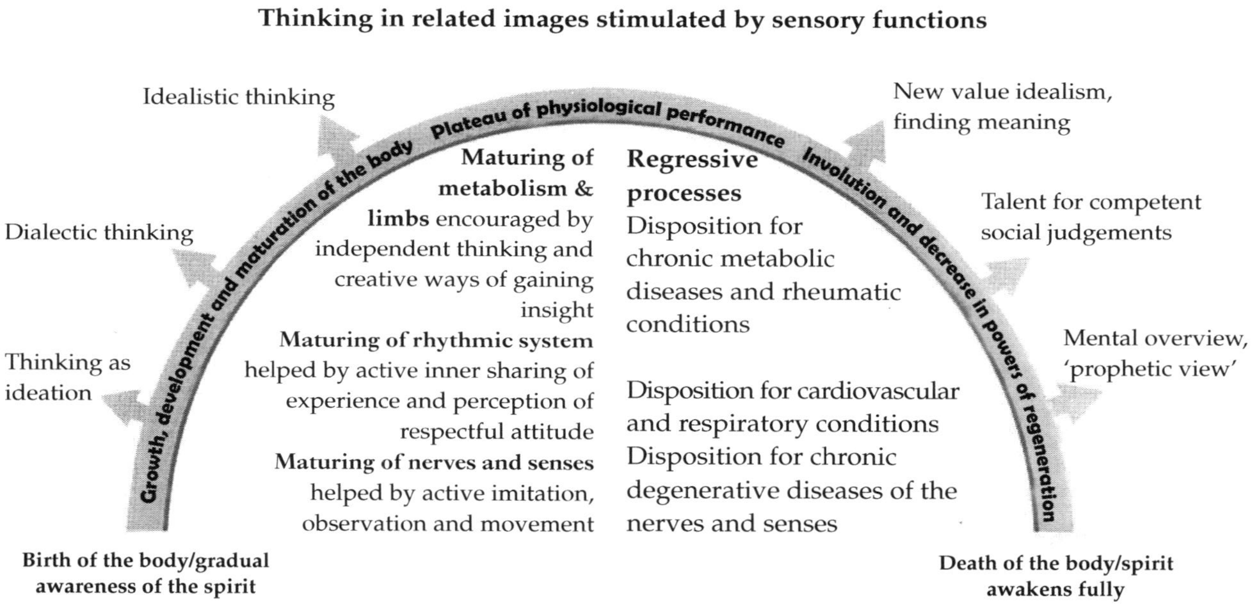

Developmental and involutional processes in the human organism and the corresponding maturation stages in thought life

At this point it is interesting that these three cardinal organ systems go through involution in reverse order in the second half of life—with concurrent development of new, creative potential in thinking, and ageing evident in signs ranging from slight degeneration to typical chronic diseases.

Women will normally go through the menopause between the 40th and 50th years of life. However, both men and women find that their energies grow less in a similar way in their metabolic organs and limbs at that time. Depending on circumstances chronic disease may also make its first appearance in these areas. This may also be a rheumatic condition, gallstones or kidney stones, metabolic syndrome or diabetes 2.

Be that as it may, people's thoughts go towards a new idealism, way of life and values are questioned. They may take up a new kind of work or have a new beginning in some other way, for they finally do wish to live their own life.

Between the 50th and the 60th year the rhythmic system begins to age. Depending on the given disposition, people develop high blood pressure and cardiac arrhythmias, lung diseases become chronic. With regard to thinking, however, there is a more objective, mature power of judgement, and the ability to reconcile opposites, able to assess them deliberately.

Between the 60th and 70th years signs of degeneration are more common in the sense organs and the central nervous system. Their onset predominates at this age, ultimately leading to chronic morbidity. It is all the more surprising that normally there is no loss of mental capacity running parallel to the physical changes. Even if the brain is demonstrably ageing, as do the sense organs, and measurably losing substance, this development may nevertheless go hand in hand with a lively mind, new perspectives and ways of seeing things. It is not only that the nervous system's plasticity and ability to compensate are retained well into old age—further creative powers are freed as these organ systems decompose. This leads to new potential for forming ideas and a greater ability to gain an overview even if short-term memory will sometimes let one down a bit. This is different, of course, if dementia develops. This, however, is not healthy ageing but a disease of the nervous system. Yet even in this case one has to take it that the powers of thought, feeling and will are very much 'all there'. It is just that healthy brain function is no longer there to provide a basis for developing thoughts, feelings and will impulses in a self-aware and orderly way. It is therefore all the more important to develop new kinds of communication, taking into account this spiritual aspect, which is a reality, and the individual concerned being able to sense this.

Human development clearly is not linear but is a mirror image around the middle of biological life. It shows that the way in which development proceeded in childhood and youth determines the severity of chronic conditions and signs of wear and tear in old age. If we take this point of view, a new, very real insight is gained into primary prevention and prophylaxis. These appear primarily to be a matter of education (see page 47ff.)—the sounder the process of incarnation, i.e. of growth and development, has been in childhood and youth, the more harmonious can the process of involution, of ageing, or excarnation be. Waldorf education is committed to the concept of education serving prevention and based on this the promotion of health. Because of this, the vocation of a kindergarten and school doctor as seen by Rudolf Steiner also involves playing an important role among the teaching staff and in everyday school life.[71,72,73,74]

It also touches one deeply to come across descriptions of near-death experiences in this context. All of them say that when a person is near death—be it from shock, trauma or an operation—he suddenly sees himself as if from above and is able to move out of the body. As if the greatest part of mortal life in the body had changed into bright, everlasting life in thought, feeling and will.[75] The individual has an out-of-body experience independent of spatial limitations. The process of dying, as seen in terms of the body, is in mind and spirit felt to be a new birth for a life in the spirit. Pim van Lommel, a cardiologist with extensive insight into his patients' out-of-body experiences, created the term 'infinite consciousness'.[76,77]

Health and sickness

Health is not the absence of disease but rather the outcome of daily coming to terms with the damage caused to the organism and the potential for compensation. The greater the powers of self-healing and immunocompetence, the more robust the state of health. Sickness and healing are opposites. Health is the unstable balance between them. Whatever the harmful influences coming from the environment, caused by mental stress or also by autoaggression, the organism will only grow sick if it is unable to oppose those influences with enough constructive, healing activities.

Why do people fall ill? That is the question asked by the two founders of anthroposophic medicine in the second chapter of *Extending Practical Medicine*, the book they wrote together.[79] The answer is as clear as it is surprising. People get ill because they are not only part of the natural world but also have an individual life in soul and spirit.

Animals do also have souls but do not have an individualized, self-aware life in mind and spirit, taking personal responsibility. They are not normally subject to disease. This only comes when the ecological balance is upset, and will then also soon lead to the death of the affected creatures. Animals are only taken to the vet by human beings. Anthroposophic veterinary medicine has developed on this basis.[80,81,82] In the natural world, the ecological balance maintains species and ensures a rapid death if that balance is upset. It is therefore in accord with the dignity of the creature and an ancient tradition to grant sick or wounded animals a rapid and as far as possible painless death. It is different when it comes to human beings. Here one does everything possible to maintain life and support the sick individual through stages of disease that may sometimes be very long. Why is that the case? People are able to go consciously through pain and suffering and so gain experiences that will take them forward in their development. Animals are helplessly exposed, having no opportunity to distance themselves or learn from the situation as they do not have powers to reflect on things.

In his book, *Childhood and Human Evolution*, zoologist Friedrich Kipp has explored this evolution-biological difference between animal and man.[83] He shows that compared to mammals, man has a typically extended childhood and youth, with a prolonged play and learning phase and that this does eminently support his ability to change and adapt throughout life.

For the way we see ourselves it is therefore also important to understand that man is not 'descended from the apes', as the Darwinian theory of evolution would have it. Phaenotypically the images of mammalian embryonic development show a different evolutional perspective: in the gestures of embryonic development, *animals are descended from man.* The forms and characteristics they show in their early stages of development are retained through life by man. Specialization in a particular animal form is a later stage. Animals develop specific body form and soul qualities, perfect for their instinct-governed way of life; human beings do not. Physicians offer most in providing medical care where the most natural aspects are concerned, for even this is not natural for us but has to be learned—to eat a healthy diet, take enough exercise and be sexually active in the way that feels right for the individuals concerned. Animals have their natural, healthy way of life by instinct. For human beings this involves central issues of human values and culture. Everyone has to discover for himself what is right for him and how he can understand the other person. Even humanity does not come naturally. It is a cultural achievement that has to be acquired and cannot be gained by instinct or by training. It will only come, and be felt to be genuine if intended and developed by individuals. And it is only human beings who learn things from being sick, things that also enable them to mature in soul by caring for the sick and by suffering weakness and pain. They thus develop new abilities, particularly social ones. In short, we may say that pain and suffering do not make any animal—dog, horse, bird or fish—'doggier', 'more horsey', 'more birdy' or 'more fishy'. Only man can grow more human by this means. It therefore makes sense that only human beings have the opportunity, e.g. to be born with diseases, live with them, learn from them and gain

Evolution of chimpanzee head from birth to sexual maturity

impulses for further development. Animals are naturally perfect in their given life form. Human beings on the other hand stay a bit childlike all their life and in a process of becoming. It is deeply moving to see how much mammals look like humans during their embryonic development and in early development after birth, as is evident in the figure above. For as long as they are still developing they show human traits. These will then rapidly disappear as the body matures to achieve the typically animal perfection and specialization based on the inborn certainty of instinct.[84]

The stages of development for a chimpanzee head and the wing of a bird clearly show resemblance to human forms the younger the animal is.

Both mammalian and avian developments show this. They only specialize in their typical animal form as their bodies mature. This means that phaenotypically they are descended from man. Initially the embryonic development of the bird's wing still shows the five rays similar to the human hand. Then the bird's flight

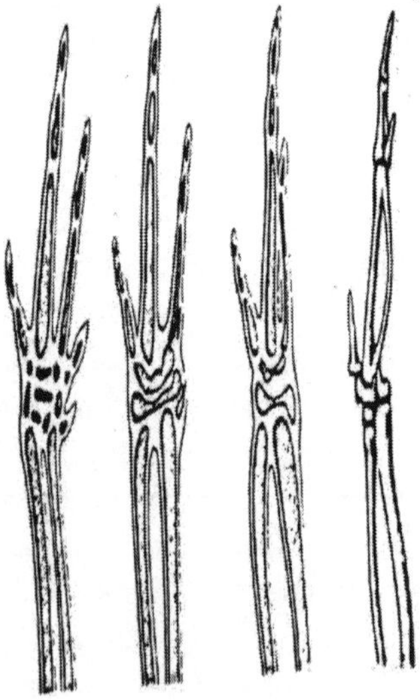

Embryonic development of a bird's wing

skeleton of the wing is differentiated out. The potential skills of the human hand have to be learned by observation and thinking. Birds need little practice for perfect flight once the wings have matured. The human body and its organs are not specialized and perfected. It needs thinking, feeling and acting out of the will, soul powers that come from outside the body. Man is, as it were, dispensing with perfection and specialization in order to retain the flexibility of a child and be able to take in something that is *in statu nascendi* and use it in a wholly nonphysical way—his own I nature, the origin of his autonomous way of becoming a self, an I.

Self-determined and free from compulsions imposed by nature, man is then able to develop what he wishes to create in technology or art. He is made for self-development. Compared to the animals his body retains an unspecialized, embryonic or infantile form. This also has consequences in education. Children who were given plenty of room for play and creativity will, as a rule, also remain flexible and creative into ripe old age. The earlier children become specialized, conditioned and schooled in kindergarten and school and thus appear to be 'set', the greater is the danger that later on they will be uncreative, adapted, age earlier and tend to be sick.

Why do people fall ill? They fall ill because they have a soul and a spirit which they must learn to handle—their development being susceptible to disorder—because they have not only been given freedom but also the potential for error. Health is 'being in harmony', signifies integration and balance. Sickness, on the other hand, shows lack of harmony, phenomena of isolation and dissociation as well as processes of disintegration.

Sleeping and waking and the development of sickness

The figure shown below indicates the way in which the ether body works during the day and at night. In the waking state the ether body serves sensory perception, the forming of ideas

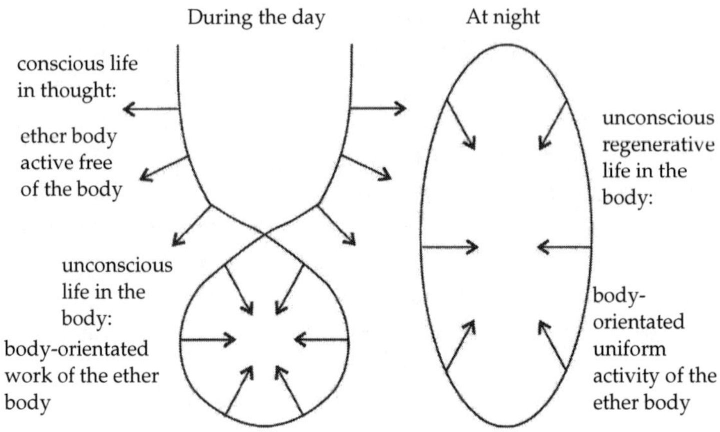

Function of the etheric body during the day and night

and thought activity, which is independent of the body. In sleep it particularly regenerates the nervous system and the sense organs, having worn them down by using them from outside to work with sensory perceptions and form ideas when awake. The rhythmic alternation of function from outside (waking) and then from inside (sleeping) is also the key for understanding how sickness arises.

If the I has been warm-hearted and enthusiastic in its daytime activities in the thought organism, it takes constructive, life-promoting after-effects of thought life with it into the night-time regeneration process. Yet if the thinking had been primarily only geared to the material things in life, relatively independent of the life of feeling, the I will take the after-effects of this thinking with it into the night.[85]

Night after night the after-effects of thought life can thus affect the body's vitality, enlivening and ordering, or in a disruptive, less lively way the regenerative processes in the body. Depending on the destiny situation, depending on constitution and circumstances, this will, however, have the additional strengthening effect which the individual concerned needs for his daily life, or they will gradually be the reason for an individually acquired destiny kind of sickness.

The meaning of typical diseases in the course of life—sickness and destiny

The next figure (p. 44) shows two human bodies on a rising and a falling arch. Both have the emphasis on the head, at the beginning and the end, with the limbs facing each other. The left, rising semi-arch shows the process in which the body matures until fully grown. The body on the right (and the right semi-arch) shows the process of ageing, of involution, all the way to death.

The three phases of the body's life: growth, best age—with regard to the body's as well as the mind and soul's level of performance—and gradual decline of the body due to ageing, go hand in hand with three groups of typical diseases. Even people who say that they have always been in perfect health do not escape entirely. Someone who may not remember having one of the impressive childhood diseases will have had a cough as a child, a runny nose, hoarseness, diarrhoea or a food intolerance. We call them minor infections because they leave no after-effects and one tends to forget about them. They are essential, however, for with them the body's developing immune system learns to cope with the environment and adapt to it. We come to terms with many bacteria and viruses without realizing it—we call this 'occult immunization'—others cause minor infections more or less in passing. Infections in childhood and the sensible use of vaccinations strengthen immunocompetence.[86,87] That is the nature-given purpose of acute infections.

We learn something different in midlife. Acute infections are no longer normal at this time. As a rule, people are now physically resilient and in good health. Typical problems are situation-related sleep disorders, problems with appetite, indigestion, shooting pains in the heart, malaise, bad moods, a feeling of weakness or lack of energy—known as psychosomatic disorders. They are typical for the time between the twentieth and fortieth year, sometimes also persisting a bit longer, for here we must learn to cope with our *psycho-social* environment at home and at work. We then find that we still have not grown immune in the psyche. We are vulnerable, open to attack and unstable.

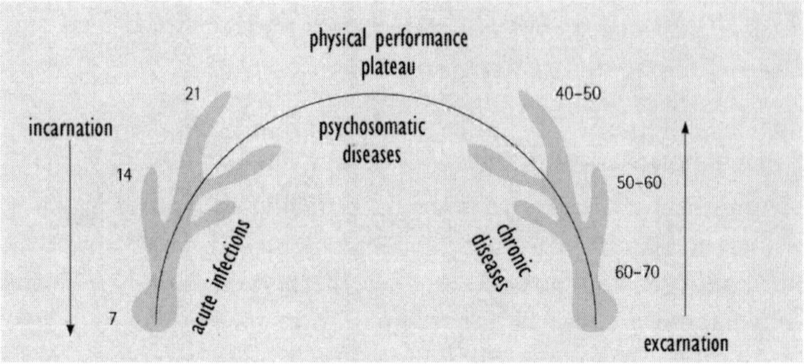

Typical biographical forms of disease

We still have not adequately learned to react appropriately to impertinence, cope with unpleasantness, learn to meet psychosocial stress with a good psychic immune system. If we go and see our doctor because of this he will either say that you are physically fit and your problems are mental in origin. Or: 'Yes, you have neurodystonia, functional symptoms, but fortunately it is nothing serious, no manifest physical sickness. But you must do something to help yourself.' Self-coaching is then indicated as well as natural medicines to give support. Anthroposophic physicians will, for instance, suggest you read Rudolf Steiner's *How to Know Higher Worlds*, a book for inner development, or that the patient goes to a biographical counsellor, art therapist or some other good lifestyle guide. For this is where the psyche must be immunized—without growing hard in the process, uncaring, and letting things take their course. If this is ignored and the necessary inner training does not take place, the individual will again and again be unwell and go through crises in life because things that need to be dealt with at soul level are somatized and are dealt with through sickness at the physical level, which is the wrong place. The most common cause of dependence on tablets, so widespread today, will be found there. Sleeping tablets, painkillers, tablets for nausea, headache tablets, tablets inducing euphoria, a high, tablets to help concentration—all come under this heading. Symptomatic medicines replace the necessary self-development. Unfortunately this means that damage due to undesirable side effects is accepted and so are rising health costs.

The third stage in life, shown as the descending arch in the above figure, shows the onset and localization of the typical chronic diseases of old age (see page 36ff. This triggers a mental and spiritual learning process which is not easy to describe.

Someone suffering from a chronic disease will come to know the feeling 'From now on you will never again be fully fit.' To the end of your life you will be sick, limited or at least slightly impaired. With a bit of humour one might say that chronic diseases are our best friends, for they remain faithful to us until we take our last breath. The story 'The Messengers of Death', recorded by the brothers Grimm, tells of this. In the end it emerges that the chronic diseases were the messengers warning of death, wanting that one prepared for the end of one's life in good time. At this stage of life we are concerned with mental and spiritual immunization. Moving towards death and the time after death, I come to see one thing. My individual body and also my inner experiences that were made possible by that body will vanish at death. My soul and spirit—with thinking, feeling and doing—must in foreseeable time manage to cope in the out-of-body world. From now on I must also gain my mental and spiritual bearings. To understand what it means when one no longer gains experiences in a physical body that has grown familiar is a similarly dramatic metamorphosis—only the other way round—as the slow habituation process that took one from the spiritual world which one lived in before birth through conception, birth and childhood to identification with one's own body. The poet Novalis once said that the death of a spirit is the birth of a body; and when a body dies, a spirit is born.

Someone who has during life on earth given thought to out-of-body experiences in the soul, eternal conscious awareness or life eternal after death, can face this step across the boundary of life in the world perceived through the senses with equanimity. If this does not happen, one will be in danger of being afraid of death, or to content oneself with the idea that it will be the end of everything anyway. Chronic diseases evoke this inner process of coming to terms. Those who avoid them are more likely to reach for the bottle or get used to the diversions always available through the entertainment industry. They fail to make their own mental and spiritual development potential a regular part of their life. Yet when we think of this potential, which everyone has even if they take no interest in it, we learn to immunize ourselves in mind and spirit. Moving towards death then becomes a spiritual maturing process that comes to a temporary end with the birth in the spirit as we die. The poet, Rainer Maria Rilke (1875–1927) wrote a prayer for this.

Lord, let each have his own death.
Dying that comes from a life
Where he knew love, meaning and pain.

For we are but the shell and the leaf.
The great death, which each has within him,
That is the fruit around which all revolves.[88]

In Christian terms this means 'Blessed are the dead which die in the Lord from henceforth.'[89] Or, 'He who does not die before he dies will perish when he dies.'[90] Just as there is the first birth from the mother's womb and the second birth 'of water and of the spirit',[91] so there is also the death of the body and that of self-awareness—death of the soul. It means that after death the soul loses its spiritual awareness and 'sleeps' until it becomes embodied again and awakens to self-awareness by activity of the self in the body. It means that those who do not make the effort to develop an individual awareness of their spiritual existence will also not be able to take this across the threshold of death (see page 21).

Apart from the three groups of typical diseases in old age—acute, psychosomatic, chronic—there are also 'destiny-related' diseases that are not typical for old age. They usually come unexpectedly, sometimes beginning before birth. They seem to belong to the personal destiny which one feels to be inevitable;

it confronts one and has meaning only if one can consider it against the background of a positive understanding of destiny.

Destiny and reincarnation

In the study mentioned earlier Bernd Rosslenbroich showed that the evolution of species is subject to a common principle that culminates in the evolution of man. It is the principle of progressive autonomy. This also relates to man's dilemma. Human beings are made for freedom but at every step they take they discover how hard it is to make constructive, self-determined use of this freedom. Again and again we know powerlessness, dependence, or realize too late that we have made the wrong decision. We wish for what we do not have, it being certain that we shall not attain to it in this life on earth. Or we are unable to make proper use of a gift we have. We may have many degrees of freedom but much does not succeed or there is no joy to our achievements because we really wanted to achieve something else. This one life on earth is limited and does, at every step, make us aware of our own limitations. Emil Bock was the first to look for individuals in (central) European civilization who were convinced that human beings live more than once. He found this view—irrespective of faith—in all who had thought a great deal about the fact that people develop individually.[92]

What fascinated Bock was that everybody who realizes that human beings develop not only in body but also in soul and spirit must sooner or later find that for this reason alone one life on earth can never be enough to become fully human, or oneself. It needs a great number of very different lives to come close to the degree of freedom, dignity, self-respect, understanding, tolerance, social competence and empathy that is needed to make one truly a good person. For what do we know about being human if we have lived only once, as man or woman, if one has been close to nature, in a large city, in poverty or riches, if one had a management post, was an unskilled worker, in one vocation or another, or out of work? How far is one a qualified human being after one life as a scientist, artist or engaged in the business world—creating culture or destroying the environment—in times of war or peace? And what about belonging to a particular religious community or not belonging to any community with shared values? All these conditions of life and destiny mean that certain human abilities can develop and others not.

Compared to the animal world with its species, every human being has his own particular way of existing and developing—because he has his own, unique destiny. This even holds true for identical twins who have the same genotype and usually have also grown up in the same environment. Their destinies differ in spite of this. They live with different partners, often also in different locations and in different occupations, and so on. Their own destiny makes them into this one, particular human being, the only one among 7,000 million people on earth. So with everyone having the right, indeed the obligation, to develop as a human being, to be truly human, there also has to be the continuation and further development of destiny elements through many lives. This also means, however, that in experiencing our destiny we are ultimately alone, however many friends and acquaintances we may have. For no one has exactly the same experiences and existence as we do.

This means that we ourselves have a clear indication that we are made for autonomy. The sense of isolation that comes with a unique destiny that has to be lived through individually may be painful but it makes us aware that ultimately we have to rely on our conscience, that inner voice, if we want to keep our freedom and not be dependent on family, friends, advisers and authorities. We then also owe it to this potential for freedom that we can stand alone, withdrawing or also overcoming others with our powers of persuasion, often hurting or causing damage to others without realizing it.

It is evident, therefore, that destiny events and the existence of our unique individual I nature can also have painful consequences for us. Again and again we find ourselves facing the consequences of our actions in this or a later life, things we have done to others and to our environment. These consequences may be evident in our own body, in our inner life, or through destiny events where we do not immediately understand the causes and therefore speak of 'accidents' or 'chance'. This means that not only our capacity for freedom will have opportunity to develop but also the social side of the I's competence—selfless love. In the Gospels, these opportunities and risks are put in profound words. In Matthew 10: 34–37 we read: 'Do not suppose that I came to bring peace on the earth. I did not come to bring peace but a sword. As I came to cause disagreement between a man and his father, a daughter and her mother, a bride and her mother-in-law, [...] The one who cares for father or mother more than for me is not worthy of me. [...] The one who does not take his cross and follow after me is not worthy of me.' Yet in the same Gospel we also read that we should love our enemies, do good to those who hate us, bless those who curse us, pray for those who insult us.[93] The Sermon on the Mount reveals the other side of freedom. No one must react—the ancient karma principle of 'an eye for an eye, a tooth for a tooth' belongs to the past. It guided people into individualization and separateness. The new destiny or karma principle can understand, forgive and redeem one's own guilt and that of others. It comes into force through the power of the higher self which is common to all. The power is best brought into play by practising it in social life as unconditional interest in the concerns and problems of the world in which we live. This unconditional interest is a form of spiritual love—that is evident—and the precondition is that we gain autonomy. For we must feel inwardly free to let go of all justifiable fury about someone, about an enemy who has done us harm. To understand our enemy and on the basis of this understanding also be able to forgive, it needs this unconditional interest, the purest autonomic competence of the I.

In his novel *Henry of Ofterdingen* Novalis put this in the form of a talk about conscience between Sylvester, a physician, and Henry.[94] Henry asks, 'When will it no longer need any shock, any pain and any evil in the universe?'

'When there is but one power—the power of conscience. When nature has grown chaste and moral. Evil has but one cause—the general weakness, and this weakness is nothing but limited moral receptivity and freedom lacking in charm.'

Novalis' 'conscience' here is the quality of presence of mind which enables one to do what is helpful, liberating in any situation. In Steiner's *Philosophy of Spiritual Activity* it is called 'moral intuition'.[95]

Human destiny is closely connected with the physical constitution, the physical body, the etheric (life) and the astral (soul) (see page 32).[96] The I organization, which supports the I, is not subject to the limits set to these levels of human existence. Because of this, the potential for freedom is bound up with the human being's competence as an I. The voice of conscience becomes accessible from this source spring for the I, as does the inner possibility to face one's destiny freely and, as far as possible, configure it autonomously. The better the result, the greater the power to understand destiny, configure and harmonize it, for instance to heal the wounds from the past. Many painful experiences lie in a human being's past destiny but also the wisdom to be gained from them. The understanding and healing of destiny come from the future, from evolution's goal of autonomy and love. Rudolf Steiner brought both of these out in his investigations of karma so that teachers, therapists and physicians in particular would, out of this central perspective of development, be able to support young people, advise and help them in sickness and need.

Michael Bauer (1871–1929), teacher and anthroposophist, once wrote,'The idea of re-embodiment is a postulate of love. Those who truly want to help will need more than one life on earth before they grow tired.'

The following poem is by his friend Christian Morgenstern.

We must over and again meet ourselves
And over and again suffer through one another
Until one day we shall bless it all.

On that day pain will be gone,
The pain that came from self-seeking,

The pain, at least, that made us blind
Bending us in the gale like blind woodland.
Then we shall come together like rivers in an ocean,
Setting a new goal and life,
And separation shall no longer trouble us.
Then, at last, the '... seek not your own'
Will be the truth in our souls.
And we'll not lack strength nor lack good fortune.[97]

Education for individual and social health

Rudolf Steiner made a strong point when he said: 'The social question is an educational issue, and the educational issue is a medical one.'[98] It means that to cope with social problems we need an education that makes us peaceable. The precondition for such an education is that one knows the conditions under which the development of individual and social health becomes possible.

In future, Rudolf Steiner said, physicians would have to be health experts and teach individual and social health.[99] Teachers, on the other hand, should be expected to be physicians, expert in preventive methods for children. Steiner referred to teaching as a way of 'gentle healing'.[100] Together with physician Ita Wegman he sent a circular to the young physicians and medical students in March 1924, between the two further training courses at Christmas and Easter, with the following verse to inspire close collaboration of physicians and teachers.

In early days the thought
Lived strongly in the souls of the initiates
That human beings were all sick by nature.
Education was seen to be the healing process

That gave health to the maturing child
That he be wholly human in that life.[101]

Today education and therapy face four particularly great challenges:

- — the tendency to be dependent, with addiction a disease suffered by many children and young people;
- — the fact that more and more people walk past one another without taking an interest, do not understand one another. The consequences are social isolation, a sense of meaninglessness and hatred;
- — the digital revolution with the risk of losing reality, addictive behaviour and inability to learn to think independently;
- — paralysis of the will in view of the excessive information available. Talk about everything—yes, but it is difficult to concentrate and actually bring something of that excess to realization.

What form should education take so that it can effectively counteract this? How can we prevent the fourfold danger of losing autonomy, social relationships, individual access to spirituality and progressive paralysis of the will? It is evident that there lie the causes of many social and also health problems. There is urgent need to support a system of education where one is aware of the child's individual developmental situation and takes account of it in deciding on teaching methods and the curriculum. In particular it needs adults who are examples of autonomy in their thinking and actions, taking a holistic view of the world.

The children should be stimulated at every age and given opportunity to develop their own activities. That is the archetypal impulse of Waldorf education. Rudolf Steiner put it like this: 'Education is always self-education, and as teachers and educators we are really only the environment for the child who educates himself. We must be the best possible environment so that the child educates himself when with us as he must do because of his inmost destiny.'[102] Children each bring their own destiny with them and need to experience and take up whatever is right for them as individuals. It therefore needs a rich and varied range of educational material suitable for the given age so that every child can experience and take up what is appropriate for him or her.[103]

When the first Waldorf School was established, there were a number of war orphans among the children. Many of the children were undernourished, and Eugen Kolisko, the school doctor, therefore compounded roborant medicines for them. Two of them, still known today, are Calcium Supplement 1 and 2, and another 'source of nutrient power' is a supplement rich in minerals. Times were difficult following the end of World War 1. Waldorf education had integrated trauma therapy, using educational measures, in its concept from the beginning. Bernd Ruf made it known again a few years ago with his trauma-education emergency service organized with the help of Freunde der Erziehungskunst.[104]

As preventive medicine, Waldorf education is based on five basic anthroposophic principles:

1) a positive influence on the physical body by cultivating the senses (see below);
2) supporting the ether body by cultivating the rhythms and a curriculum appropriate to the age;
3) cultivation of the astral body by establishing good personal relationships with the pupils and their parents;
4) activating the pupil's I by taking a genuine interest, always developed in a new way again, in the subject which the teacher must represent to the pupils in a fully authentic way;
5) with a spiritual orientation one lives with in full awareness that gives pupils the confidence that one day they, too, will be firm, strong characters and find their own way to a well-founded identity.

Cultivating the senses in a digital age

Rudolf Steiner referred not only to the known five or seven senses but identified twelve areas of sensory perception that need to be taken into account when working with children and young people.[105] Below, an indication is given of the significance which this has for practice today, seeing that the cultivation of the sensory modalities is progressively decreasing in this digital age.

It is a blessing for physical and mental development if children are not permitted to use tablets and smartphones in the first nine years of life, and are only used in school from age 15 onwards.[106,107] For how is a sound neurosensory system to develop when digital impressions have to be digested in the most important years of development, impressions that address only eye and ear, with all other senses shut out, and, what is more, do not provide real interaction with the environment? Quite apart from the fact that it has been shown that the development of empathy is precluded in this case. In the digital age, education means primarily to provide protection against premature use of the media and thus make a real contribution to preserving childhood. Children are not small adults, even if one can apparently seduce or condition them in this direction. They need a childhood with much activity of their own and the joy of making discoveries, and a youth when the necessary self-finding processes can take place and the development of firm relationships is supported.

The function of the senses does not only permit differentiated perception of the complex world we live in but also serves personal experience in living with one's own body. Experiencing self and world determine one another and promote sound identity development. The potential contribution of individual senses is listed below. For adults, deliberate training and care of the senses are a form of meditation and of finding oneself. For this, all attention and concentration focuses on a particular object for a time. Practised in this way it may, in time, also become one's all-embracing attitude. Do what you do in the right way, deliberately leaving other things aside. For children, being with adults who are able to concentrate is the best example for gaining this ability by imitation.

Sense of touch

Its organ:

— tactile cells and free nerve endings

It conveys:

— experience of self in the body boundary when touched with respect
— feeling of security, safety, especially in early childhood, sure of existence.

Suggestions as to care:

— harmonious alternation between being alone and being safe and secure
— child able to let go and 'be by himself' is just as important as 'togetherness' and 'comforting, a hug'
— from earliest childhood create spaces where the child can touch, examine and discover for himself.

Sense of life

Its organ:

— autonomous nervous system.

It conveys:

— being at ease
— feeling healthy
— contentment.

Suggestions as to care:

— regular meal and bed times
— pleasant atmophere at meals
— confident approach to life
— order and structure given to the day
— meaningful activities.

Sense of one's own movements

Its organ:

— muscle spindles.

It conveys:

— perception of one's own movement
— experiencing freedom of movement
— experiencing self control due to control of one's movements.

Suggestions as to care:

— give children opportunity to move wholly 'of their own accord' and take initiative to act
— create spaces where they can move freely at no danger
— make room for discovery and independent activity from curiosity
— arrange children's rooms and if possible the house or flat so that everything may be touched and free play is possible
— perception of meaningful targeted movement sequences
— going for walks and playing in the open air, allowing time when a child learns, discovers something, investigates, etc. Observe the child and his doings with interest and careful attention.

Sense of balance

Its organ:

— semicircular canals in region of inner ear.

It conveys:

— experiencing the search for and finding of balance
— experiencing balance as a state of rest.

Suggestions as to care:

- — movement games
- — see-saw
- — stilts
- — jumping
- — running, balancing
- — adult calm and sure when with a child.

Sense of smell

Its organ:

- — mucosa in root of nose.

It conveys:

- — being connected with the aroma as immediate substance-matter perception
- — intimate recognition of people and objects because of their smell.

Suggestions as to care:

- — always make sure air is fresh, neutral
- — take note of differentiated odours
- — look for everyday smells, e.g. when cooking, from plants and goods, when buying flowers or going on a walk.

Sense of taste

Its organ:

- — taste buds in mucosa of tongue: sweet, sour, salty, bitter.

It conveys:

- — together with sense of smell differentiated taste sensations
- — but also aesthetic sensations, like being able to smell (taste) something or someone in the sense of liking or not.

Suggestions as to care:

— preserve the particular taste of foods by suitable preparation, as far as possible avoiding taste powders and the like and synthetic aromas
— 'tasteful' judgement of people and things
— aesthetic arrangement of surroundings.

Sense of sight

Its organ:

— eye.

It conveys:

— experience of light and colours.

Suggestions as to care:

— looking at something together with the child, be amazed, delighted, especially in the natural world
— note subtle differences in colour in the natural world, happy to look oneself and letting the child share in one's own concentration
— harmonious colours in clothing and furnishings
— things seen every day need special attention: it 'makes sense' and 'does you good'
— game: I see something which you don't see ...

Sense of temperature

Its organ:

— temperature receptors in the skin and mucosa.

It conveys:

— experience of hot and cold.

Suggestions as to care:

- natural textiles for clothing to care for warmth organism
- producing a good atmosphere with warmth of soul and spirit
- avoiding premature toughening measures that are not wanted by the child himself.

Sense of hearing

Its organ:

- inner ear.

It conveys:

- experience of sound
- bringing inner soul space to conscious awareness.

Suggestions as to care:

- singing
- playing the lyre, learning to hear also slight sounds
- listening to classical music and if possible also learning to play it
- when telling or reading stories adapt rate of speech to the child's ability to take things in
- when telling/reading stories stop again and again, pause so that inner images and sound or tone memory may develop.

Sense of language (word)

Its organ:

- develops through perception of movement sequences, mime and processes of gaining awareness of speech.

It conveys:

- experience of configuration and physiognomy (sense of configuration)

— grasping body language
— grasping the meaning of the configuration of sounds in a word.

Suggestions as to care:

— warm, kind voice
— paying attention to gestures and body language
— inner life in full accord with what one is saying
— honesty—the senses do not lie. Young children are aware of what we think and feel even if our words say something else.

Sense of thought

Its organ:

— develops with the complex perception of life's events.

It conveys:

— immediate comprehension of connection between thoughts or a sequence of actions
— understanding the way thoughts relate even if a word is the wrong one or the context is merely hinted at.

Suggestions as to care:

— practise uprightness and harmony in dealing with oneself and others
— establish relationships between things and between events
— maintain meaningful order, avoid chaotic thinking and actions.

Sense of self (of I)

Its organ:

— develops on touch and contact perception in the boundary of one's own body, to be organ for complete perception of another individual.

It conveys:

- direct experience and recognititon of the other individual as I-endowed.

Suggestions as to care:

- truly perceive the other individual, taking an interest in him
- again and again give one's attention to every member of the family
- show pleasure in the other individual
- cultivate a culture of encounter and visiting.

Anyone wishing to learn more about the anthroposophical theory of the senses may refer to further literature on the subject.[108,109]

Parents look at a newborn infant in a very different way if they do not think 'We have made you' but realize 'We have provided the seed for your bodily development, but you have given it the form it will need for your life.' Respect for the body's integrity and the dignity of every individual human being is the foundation of education for true humanity and a medicine that bears a human face.

This basic attitude is particularly important towards children, but also older people, confused and weak individuals and people needing extra support. Anthroposophic education for special needs, social therapy, palliative medicine and care of the sick and the aged have developed exemplary methods for this.[110,111,112] Anthroposophic medicine here often finds itself in conflict with the spirit of modern materialistic medicine. The latter does not have a concept for understanding, supporting and adequately helping such forms of life. To recognize pain and suffering in their significance for the development of the human mind and spirit is not to glorify this dark side of human existence. It means rather that the messages of suffering must also be integrated into development. Pain and suffering wake us up, give conscious awareness—happiness and joy on the other hand give strength, 'lend wings'. Both are vital to us. The idea of destiny and reincarnation also should not induce us to minimize or indeed justify problems or weaknesses. But it can give impulses to give a form worthy of humanity to whatever life has to offer and, in the best possible way, learn from this for our further development. In palliative care, great value therefore attaches to maintaining the sick individual's dignity right to the end, supporting his quality of life.[113,114,115] The focus is always on the human *spirit* 'which builds its own body' and also destroys it again, ageing sooner or more slowly, continuing its development in life after death.

Today's ethical questions, like those connected with organ transplantation or in-vitro fertilization, have to be true to life and realistic. It is not a question of 'for' or 'against' but of understanding what is happening there in body and spirit, and then to make a decision that is as free as possible, with consequences one will be able to live with as a self-determined person.[116,117]

When it comes to the 'ethics of dying' one must, however, endeavour to make the meaning of old age and the value of life, of every hour spent on earth, come alive. Suicide and assisted death are seen as acts of desperation and must be prevented. The ethical basis of anthroposophic medicine is to promote life to the end, using the means of social culture and a holistic medicine.[118,119,120]

Anthroposophic physicians are not against vaccination, although this is often said to be the case.[121] It is rather that they are for deciding on vaccination in the individual case, taking care that the child's development of immunity is not compromised.[122,123,124]

Rudolf Steiner did not create the concept of salutogenesis. That was done by the American medical sociologist Aaron Antonovsky (1923–1994). Steiner never spoke on education or medicine without considering the healthy human being, the potential for whom exists in every human being, and to show how that potential can be strengthened. Modern research on salutogenesis is thus referring to many things which are in agreement with Rudolf Steiner's investigations of health and his suggestions for the practical application of the results. In the same way the findings in hygiogenesis, salutogenesis and resilience studies as well as the representatives of positive psychotherapy and logotherapy after Viktor Frankl have clearly shown and substantiated the importance of positive acceptance of the sound part of everyone's mind and spirit to support healing.[125,126,127]

With his concept of salutogenesis, Aaron Antonovsky clearly left his mark on twentieth-century health investigation. He looked for the conditions under which health develops—salus, from the Latin, means 'health', genesis, from the Greek, 'development, origin'—and made sense of coherence the core concept, i.e. a sense of being in accord, or cohesion. He found that people are all the more healthy the more they feel in tune with their environment and with themselves. This coherence can be induced in three ways. In one's thinking and sensory perceptions by things being comprehensible; in one's feeling life by their being meaningful; at the level of our actions by finding them manageable, feasible. He referred to conditions for developing this sense of coherence in the form of the right kind of education and self education, saying that it was necessary for everyone to develop a philosophy of life that would later enable them to work through the events of their life so that they make sense. This, he said, would be the best preconditions for not falling ill. Waldorf education is, in its suggestions for teaching methods, consistently geared to these goals which Antonovsky demands. Rudolf Steiner put this most clearly when speaking of independent Christian religion lessons for children, not confessionally or religiously committed, in the setting of the Sunday service for children. The words are:

> We learn so that we may understand the world.
> We learn so that we may work in the world.
> Love of one individual for another enlivens all human efforts.
> Without love human existence grows lifeless and desolate.
> The Christ teaches us human love.[128]

To put this into practice continues to be a great challenge in teacher training. For the teacher must work on himself in this sense of salutogenesis, otherwise he cannot be an example and convey this through his teaching.

Some examples will show this.

- *To be comprehensible.* Many inner problems come from a deep down feeling of inadequacy, being unable to understand something—for instance mathematics—in school or 'never' having understood it. Feeling one does not understand also means loss of some of one's self-esteem, and this can become morbid. Conversely this feeling of impotence and failure to comprehend makes one uncritical in admiring others, inclined to think that they are able 'to see through it all'. This can lead to illusions and dependence on others, something which also does not promote health. The individual concerned does not want to make the effort to develop his own powers of judgement and because of this fails to develop further. Life and health however *are* development, change, liveliness. If a teacher is aware of these problems he will be able to support his students, learning *from them* how best to do this, and that is exactly where students are apt to have a block. The more he gets interested in those individual blocks the better will the teacher be able to help, understanding and resolving the problem.

- *Meaningfulness.* Not everything we understand does also seem meaningful to us. How many dreadful things happen hour after hour around the globe—owing to the infinitely tragic deficits in education and development. It is hard to find meaning. It needs a wide developmental perspective, across generations, to manage it. In an epigram Goethe put it like this: 'Anyone who cannot account for himself over a period of 3,000 years will remain inexperienced in the dark, may just live from day to day.'[129] It is not self-indulgent to occupy oneself with meaning issues, nor is it merely to find comfort or wishful religious thinking. The point is that repeated experience of powerlessness and meaninglessness damages one's health. It therefore needs a very real, motivated search for meaning, most easily set alight by genuine interest in people and history. It is not only individual people and social conditions that change but also humanity as a whole. To be coherent with humanity and its historical development is beneficial. Someone who is unable to be a grateful child of his time lacks an important health factor. That is why schools need to have more history lessons again and not only social studies. It should, however, be history taught not (only) by memorizing dates and events, but geared to the study of the great civilizations and periods of development humanity has known. Considering the question as to what became of these, may also offer possibilities for identifying with humanity as a whole. Meaningfulness is always experienced when something that happens or that one knows about can be given its right place and so have meaning for *oneself*. Life always proceeds in a surrounding world which we share. If one is able to find this meaningful, one will feel at peace. Not to be at peace is one of the most common reasons for the abuse of drugs and medicines.

- *Manageability*. The point is that when one has understood something and it makes sense one can also have the feeling: If I wanted to, I would support it, could contribute to it or even do it myself. The sense of incapacity, of powerlessness, one's own unfitness makes one ill. But we gain in health if we know our capacities and whenever possible make them grow. Mental effort, thinking along with others, intercessions and good wishes are also part of this. We can do much more in soul and spirit than we can outwardly do if we feel ourselves to be connected with people who are doing important things and let our good thoughts be with them.

Abraham Maslow was asking himself what represented mental health. He found that people in the healthiest general mental state differed in many respects from the average population. They were pragmatic rather than self-seeking, able to take real pleasure in things, also to be amazed, and to develop feelings of devotion. In one way or another they were all following a spiritual path and would on occasion also have a peak experience. That is a direct encounter or being in touch with the spiritual that would spread light and warmth over the whole of life and lead to absolute trust in the spiritual world and its power to sustain. Near-death experiences are also part of this (see page 38). Maslow was thus able to show the high degree to which work on one's own personal development had a positive effect on the whole of one's state of health.[130]

Viktor Frankl on the other hand made the question of *meaning* the basic theme of all health-giving psychotherapy, giving quite specific expression to this in his logotherapy.[131] Hans Jonas, ethics philosopher, asked in his book, *The Imperative of Responsibility* that, considering that the earth as our sphere of life was under

Abraham Maslow
(1908–1970)

Aaron Antonovsky
(1923–1994)

Viktor Frankl
(1905–1997)

Hans Jonas
(1903–1993)

increasing threat of being destroyed by technology and force of arms, modern people wake up and as individuals share responsibility. If this does not happen social harm and destructive processes will be the inevitable consequence.

Using the concept of the metamorphosis of the levels of human existence (see page 32) it is furthermore possible to show *how and why, or by what psychosomatic pathways* the sense of coherence or the peak experience can have a positive effect on physical health. It is too easy to say that well-being or a feeling of trust or confidence is generated by neurotransmitters from the group of endorphins and oxytocins. This ignores the fact that well-being hormones and oxytocins are only created in the process of peak experience and active memory of it. Administering existing or manufactured hormones does, of course, have a temporary medicinal effect. It does not, however, change the person's character. And when the effect of a medicine or drug dies away the old, unsatisfactory condition returns, more painful than ever. In the same way it must continue to be incomprehensible why a depression can change quite suddenly when someone very dear to one, a person one trusts, turns up unexpectedly. Such an unexpected meeting can be of more lasting benefit than an antidepressant.

Thomas Fuchs, Heidelberg neurologist and neuropsychiatrist, has impressively shown in his pioneering book, *Ecology of the Brain: The phenomenology and biology of the embodied mind* how the brain develops from life for life.[132] Goethe had, in his day, realized that 'the eye develops from light for light'. Every organ needs its particular activity in and from the environment, the right stimulus that will permit its healthy development. Walther Buehler (1913–1995) wrote a much-read small volume *Living with Your Body*.[133] With their neuronal networks and transmitter substances the brain and the sense organs result from the quality of human relationships and the way in which the individual experiences life.

Anthroposophic Medicines

The anthroposophic pharmacopoeia includes about 2,000 natural substances, compound preparations and a large number of formulations: ampoules, eye drops, dilutions, emulsions (oily), diluted fluids, fluids for inhalation, fluids for external application, gels, injections, capsules, lotions, metal mirror foils, mixtures, nose drops, oils, pastes, plasters, powders, dusting powders, ointments (low fat), ointments, syrup, tablets, teas, tinctures for external use, triturations, drops, vaginal globules, vaginal tablets, aqueous dilutions, suppositories.

One important principle for the action of medicines made from plants has its basis in the threefold nature of man and plant (see the figure on the next page).

Human beings take up nourishment—in the form of foods, or as food for the soul or spirit in the form of thoughts, and words, facts from the arts and sciences through the head. The plant takes up the nutrients it needs through its roots. The opposite is true for the reproductive region. In the plant it is up above, open to air and light; in human beings it is positioned downwards and inwards. What the two have in common is that gas exchange takes place at the centre—via the leaves in plants, via the rhythmic functions of respiration and circulation in humans—although the process is again the other way round. Plants are able to develop a carbon skeleton and give off oxygen; human beings take in oxygen, degrade the carbon skeletons of foods and exhale the carbon as carbon dioxide.

The use of roots therefore supports and heals in case of diseases affecting the head and the nerves and senses. That has also been the tradition with natural and folk medicine. Teas made with the leaves are indicated for disorders of the rhythmic functions—especially heart and lung conditions. Medicines made from fruits stimulate metabolic and digestive processes.

The same relationships apply when it comes to our diet. Those who see to it that the proportion of roots, leafy vegetables, fruits and seeds are balanced, provide a diet that meets the needs of the whole body. Seeds in form of grain, nuts, sunflower seeds etc. harmonize the attunement of the three systems to one another. The active principles of the constituents are added to these basic principles.

For the medicinal use of minerals, plants and animal materials one must also consider the role which a particular chemical element or a compound such as water, salt, ash, tannins or pyrite plays in the life of nature. The signature of this function or activity also tells us what effect the substance in question may have in the human organism. To get to know the human being as a microcosm in the context of world evolution at large, with its processes and chemical relationships—its traditional name being the macrocosm—also provides the key to understanding anthroposophic medical treatment.[134,135,136]

The groups of substances from the mineral, vegetable, animal and human worlds also have a direct therapeutic connection with the levels of existence. Human matter, such as mother's milk or in the form of donated blood, supports and maintains the *physical body*. Preparations made with animal matter stimulate the *ether body* to be more active. Vegetable-based medicines,

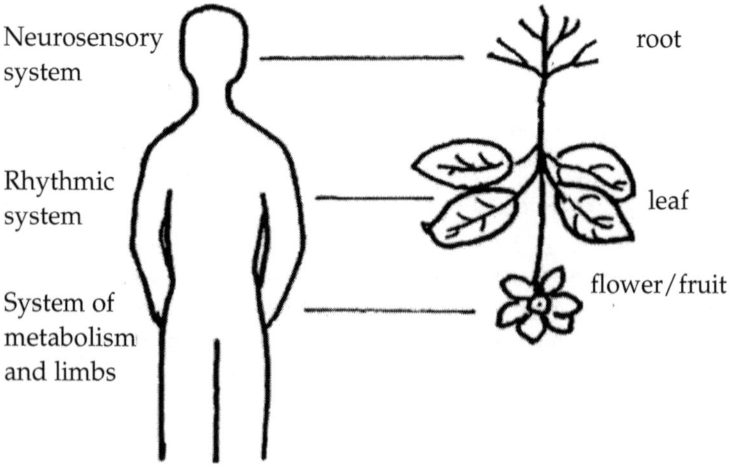

Action of plant-based medicines in human beings

on the other hand, regulate the astral body. They support the ether body so that it can offer resistance to one-sided or irregular activities of the astral body. Metals and minerals provide the basis on which the *I organization* can unfold its activities in the body. It needs the solidity of minerals to be able to be its own master down to the very foundations of the body.

The homoeopathic potency stages also relate to the levels of existence:

D1 – D4 (or 1x – 4x)

Uptake into the physical organism, stimulating the coherence of its powers. In measurable concentration the substance is able to bring its inherent actions directly into play, acting at the physical substance level.

D5 – D8 (5x – 8x)

Uptake into the etheric organism, stimulating its coherence of powers. At a level of attenuation where the substances are practically no longer present in physical form the medicine has put its powers wholly at the service of the ether body via water, or in triturations via the large surface structure of lactose.

D10 – D15 (10x – 15x)

Uptake into the astral organism, stimulating the cohesion of its powers. Physical matter remains only in very small traces. Its actions can enter into the cohesion of astral powers in space and time.

D20 – D60 (20x – 60x)

Uptake into the I organization, stimulating the cohesion of its powers. The physical matter has disappeared completely and its purely spiritual action serves the I organization.

Summing up, we may say that the more the inherent physical activity recedes, the more can the substance develop its ability to serve higher spheres of activity such as life, soul and spirit. This is also utilized in agriculture and animal husbandry. The preparations used to support composting, stimulate root function and configure plant forms are made at levels of attenuation that bring the action to bear in the field of physical and etheric forces.[137]

With regard to the threefold nature of the human organism shown in the above diagram, a further aspect is the following.

D1 – D6	stimulation of metabolic system
D6 – D18	stimulation of rhythmic system
D18 – D30	stimulation of neurosensory system

When making the drug diagnosis the active principles established for the given individual case are combined and applied. The anthroposophic pharmacopoeia therefore covers the relevant starting substances of mineral, vegetable and animal origin. Two pharmaceutical firms, Weleda and Wala, use special methods to manufacture the medicines from these.[138] In Germany, manufacture has been and is done according to, Commission C regulations for the licensing of pharmaceutical products. Some of these have regulative actions that make them highly suitable for self-medication.

The comprehensive work *Anthroposophische Arzneitherapie fuer Aerzte und Apotheker* (anthroposophic medical treatment for physicians and pharmacists, English translation available, apply to Medical Section at the Goetheanum) therefore also includes an extensive chapter on self-medication. Details given of diagnosis and treatment for more than 220 conditions have been provided by prominent anthroposophic physicians.

With the kind permission of the publishers (Wissenschaftliche Verlagsgesellschaft Stuttgart) the following examples come from this work.

Examples given by three anthroposophic specialist practitioners

The examples, provided by a medical specialist, a psychiatrist and a paediatrician, show both the typical and the individual aspects of the procedure. The possibilities for self-medication at home and for everyday health problems are impressive and to be recommended. The examples do however also show the limitations and the role of the anthroposophic physician.

Arterial hypertension

Matthias Girke[139]

Main idea

The prehypertension stages are not very impressive clinically yet all the more in need of treatment (e.g. borderline hypertension). Medication is not normally required to control these stages of the disease, though they do need careful monitoring. Here a holistic treatment regimen is the best option which apart from medical treatment includes eurythmy therapy, a movement therapy, art therapy and lifestyle changes. Established arterial hypertension on the other hand does, as a rule, call for a multidimensional approach which also includes controlling medication. Hypertension demonstrates that the differing signs and symptoms do in fact have a common signature which reflects the part played by spirit and soul in the pathological process. If the aim of treatment is not only to reduce the blood pressure symptomatically but to counter the pathophysiological process to lasting effect, it will be necessary to relieve the organism medically of the sclerosis process which is in the wrong place so that the astral body and I organization will once again be able to bring their physiological actions into play. With every medicine listed below it is therefore important to consider how far it will effectively counteract the pathological process. When patients report greater vitality and general subjective improvement it becomes possible to evaluate the efficacy of the treatment, also with regard to BP readings.

Medical treatment

The medicinal agents for the dynamic, inflammation-related form of arterial hypertension are Hyoscyamus and Belladonna. Belladonna takes over the inflammation-like febrile pathological process and thus frees the astral body—which in this case is active in the wrong place—for its regular function in the circulatory system (Husemann 1980)[140]. Hyoscyamus takes over the mental excitation and upset.

The configuring powers of the I organization must be strengthened to cope with the dynamics in the psyche and this may be done with Stibium. Aurum, on the other hand, harmonizes the connection of the neurosensory system with the system of metabolism and limbs.

These medicinal agents are available in the following compositions:

- *Aurum/Stibium/Hyoscyamus pilules*/Wala, 10 pilules 3 times a day
- *Aurum/Stibium/Hyoscyamus amp.*/Wala, 1 amp. s.c. up to once a day and if required.

Aurum/Stibium/Hyoscyamus is particularly effective for patients showing restlessness coming from the neurosensory system.

- *Aurum/Hyoscyamus comp. pilules*/Weleda, 10 pilules 3 times a day, or
- *Aurum/Hyoscyamus comp. amp.*/Weleda, 1 amp. s.c. up to once a day, or
- *Aurum/Belladonna comp. pilules*/Wala, 10 pilules 3 times a day,

or

- *Aurum/Belladonna comp. amp.*/Weleda,1 amp. s.c. up to once a day, or
- *Aurum Belladonna comp. dil.*/Weleda, 20 drops 3 times a day,

or

- *Aurum Belladonna comp. amp.*/Weleda, 1 amp. s.c. up to once a day, and to enhance this at the acute stage,
- *Belladonna D6 dil.*/Weleda, 20 drops 3 times a day.

To direct astral body activity back to the system of metabolism and limbs,

- *Bryophyllum 50 % trit.*/Weleda, a coffee-spoonful 3 times a day
- *Bryophyllum D1 dil.*/Weleda, 20 drops 3 times a day (if lactose-intolerant).

For hysterical constitution

Oyster shell. This is a head form which does not surround a neurosensory system, so that the world of conscious awareness does not awaken but astral activity is taken outside to a greater degree, which stabilizes the overweening emotionalism.

- *Bryophyllum D5/Conchae D7 amp.*/Weleda, 1 amp. s.c. once a day
- *Bryophyllum D5/Conchae D7 amp. 10 ml*/Weleda, i.v. or to drink as required.

The type's tendency to perspire can be improved with

- *Bryophyllum 50 % trit.*/Weleda, a coffee-spoonful 3 times a day
- *Conchae 50 % trit.*/Weleda, a coffee-spoonful 3 times a day.

Another important medicinal plant which already has a long tradition of regulating the relationship between astral body and ether body is Rauwolfia:

- *Rauwolfia serpentina D2, D3 mother tincture*/Weleda, 20 drops 3 times a day.

Mode of action

The reserpine in Rauwolfia is known to reduce noradrenaline levels in varicosities, thus releasing the transmitter into the synaptic space. This points to the sympathetic nervous system which comes to direct experience in every stress reaction and is connected with the soul world and hence the astral body which is the vehicle for it. It is not surprising, therefore, that this medicinal plant is known especially for its powers to calm the psyche and its sedative properties and is indicated also from the anthroposophic point of view.

Mistletoe deserves mention for activating the I organization and integrating it and the astral body in the metabolic system. Its slightly antihypertensive properties have been known for a long time. One action of mistletoe that is important in this context is that it has a phosphorus-like action. With its thoroughly warming action which is related to inflammation, it is able to guide the I organization and astral body to the metabolic organism. Mistletoe therapy can reduce and regulate excessive awakening, be it because of increased preponderance of the neurosensory system in arterial hypotension which is due to it functioning too powerfully, or because astral dynamics separate out too much from the organization of metabolism and movement and restlessly seek to come awake. Mistletoe will furthermore oppose and heal arteriosclerosis with its inflammatory, warming action on the organism. Attention must be paid to the circadian temperature (measured under the tongue at 7 a.m. and 4–5 p.m.). It should show a stabilizing rhythm.

The following medicines may be used as monotherapy. If the action is inadequate or getting less, the preparation used may be changed.

- *Viscum Crataegus amp.*/Wala, 1 amp. s.c. up to 3 times a wk
- *Abnoba viscum crataegi amp.* (starting with stage 6)/ Abnoba, 1 amp. s.c. up to 3 times a wk

- *Iscucin Crataegi amp.* (up to stage E)/Wala, 1 amp. s.c. up to 3 times a wk
- *Viscum Mali e planta tota 2 % amp.*/Wala, 1 amp. s.c., starting with ½ amp., up to 3 times a wk.

Rapid action with both hypertensive typologies has been reported (GAÄD, German Anthroposophic Medical Association)[141] for

- *Belladonna D6 dil.*/Weleda, 10–20 drops twice a day
- *Sympathicus Gl D30 amp.*/Wala, 1 amp. s.c. in left upper arm twice a wk to once a day.

If arterial hypertension is combined with symptoms of hyperthyroidism, e.g. latent hyperthyroidism or also symptoms resembling hyperthyroidism though changes in the thyroid are structural only:

- *Colchicum tuber (Rh) D3 dil.*/Weleda, 20 drops 3 times a day.

The aim of treatment is different with renovascular hypertension, which is determined by the neurosensory system. The astral organization is excessively forming and hardening the vascular system, acting from the nervous system, and can no longer be held in check by an adequately strong I organization. Copper is indicated. It can redirect the astral organization from excessively powerful, spasmodic action to the processes in the metabolic system:

- *Cuprum metallicum praeparatum D6 trit.*/Weleda, a coffee-spoonful 3 times a day
- *Cuprum aceticum comp. amp.*/Wala, 1 amp. s.c. up to once a day.

If arterial hypertension becomes renalized

- *Renes/Cuprum amp.*/Wala, 1 amp. s.c. up to once a day.

If constitutionally pale, sclerotic

If exhalation is partly held back and there are symptoms of dyspnoea (see separate entry),

- *Carbo Equisetum arvensis D15 amp.*/Weleda, 1 amp. s.c. once a day in the mornings.

For older patients, constitutionally grey and pale:

- *Plumbum metallicum praeparatum D12 trit.*/Weleda, a coffee-spoonful once a day in the morning, alternating (e.g. after 4 weeks) with
- *Cuprum metallicum praeparatum D6 trit.*/Weleda, a coffee-spoonful once a day in the morning.

In cases of hypertensive encephalopathy

Where memory is getting less good, positive experiences have been made with

- *Scleron tablets*/Weleda, 1 tablet twice a day, morning & evening (in four-week courses)
- If indicated a cup of birch-leaf tea with honey daily.

With arrhythmia

Cardiodoron is a basic form of medication when a hypertensive patient develops limited respiratory modulation of the heart rate or a reduction in day/night variance.

- *Cardiodoron dil.*/Weleda, 20 drops 3 times a day

or

- *Aurum/Cardiodoron comp. dil.*/Weleda, 20 drops 3 times a day

or

- *Crataegus comp. dil.*/Weleda, 20 drops 3 times a day.

External applications

For anxiety states

- *Pallasit D2 ungt.*/Weleda, apply to calves once a day and as required.

For restless heart use heart ointment cloth/einreibung with Aurum/Lavandula for its calming effect, esp. before afternoon nap and at bedtime:

- *Aurum/Lavandula comp. ungt.*/Weleda, once a day and as required.

If anginal pain is present, rosemary compresses on arms or legs are indicated. To redirect blood dynamics pushing towards the middle and upper human being, apply compress to legs of plethoric subjects (Kusserow 1992).[142]

- *Rosemary compress* (1 L of water, two bottle caps of Rosemary Bath Milk).

For disorders of warmth organism:

- *Ginger/Equisetum kidney compress*, once a day
- *Cuprum metallicum praeparatum 0.4 % ungt.*/Weleda, applied to renal area, calves, feet.

Dietary measures

An important part of treatment is an adequate diet and the freshness of foods. This goes far beyond reducing the number of calories, though this will often be required. The aim must be to energize the astral body and I organization more strongly in the metabolism. Easily digested foods, including animal substances, do not demand much effort from the metabolism, and a vegetarian diet is therefore preferable (Steiner 2005).[143] A vegetable diet also connects human beings with the imponderable cosmic powers of configuration that make plant life possible. Because of the sclerosis connected with arterial hypertension the nature of the individual has got too much into the purely earthly, ponderable powers (Ulbricht/Southgate 1991)[144]. A vegetarian diet can be regulatory and therapeutic in this case. Animal food acts in the opposite way. It takes the individual into the earthly sphere. Depending on the individual's nature and constitution, a diet with little meat and plenty of vegetables and fruit is recommended as well as the use of vegetable oils (Appel/Moore/Obarzanek, et al. 1997)[145]. If salt intake is also reduced, the antihypertensive effect is considerable and may equal weight loss by four or five kilograms.

Another important aspect is the mineral content of foods. There has been a major change in this since food production has become industrialized (Eaton/Korner 1987)[146]. Potassium is lost in the processing, for instance, whilst sodium is added as a preservative in the form of table salt. The ratio of sodium to potassium used to be 1 : 16; today it is 3 : 1. Salt intake is, however, connected with a sclerosing, form-giving action (Steiner 1991)[147]. Clinical and experimental investigations have shown that there is a relationship between increased sodium intake and left-ventricular muscle mass, elevated pulse pressure and hence increased stiffness or reduced compliance of arterial vessels. Increased salt intake is a cardiovascular risk factor even apart from the blood pressure (Klaus/Böhm/Halle/Kolloch/Middeke/Pavenstädt/Hayer 2009)[148]. Limiting salt intake is a sensible dietary measure. Increasing the potassium may furthermore result in a remarkable reduction in blood pressure. Increasing the amount of potassium in the diet gives the metabolism a tendency towards anabolism, vitalization. The calming effect is also evident in blood pressure levels.

What is more, the ratio of sodium to potassium and hence neurosensory system to metabolism and locomotor system has greater significance where cardiovascular risk is concerned than salt or potassium intake considered on their own (Cook/Obarzanek/Cutler/Billing/Rexrode/Kumanyika/Appel/Whelton 2009)[149].

Magnesium is closely related to potassium. It is found in the green leaf pigment of plants and brings light into the life of the plant world. It therefore also plays an important role in chlorophyll-associated photosynthesis. The bright magnesium flame shows that this metal relates particularly strongly to light. Reduced intracellular magnesium is connected with various sclerotic processes. The lower the level of free magnesium in the cell the higher is the blood pressure, the stiffness of vessels and also insulin resistance. Conversely magnesium cumulation can help to improve insulin sensitivity (Barbagallo/Dominguez/Galioto/Ferlisi/Cani/Malfa/Pineo/Busardo/Paolisso 2003)[150], take the higher levels of human existence into the system of metabolism and limbs and combat sclerosis.

Exercise

Physical exercise will also achieve a marked reduction in blood pressure. The quality of movement is, however, most important here. Two basic qualities may be distinguished in a person's capacity for movement.

With isometric contraction one moves towards increasing hardening of muscle and a considerable increase in muscle tone. A movement pattern develops that is seriously congested and almost in spasm, not permitting any real movement apart from muscle tension. Then there is flowing, continuous physical movement with changing tone and tensing. The hardening quality of the neurosensory system is easily evident in isometrically tensed contraction. Its opposite is the dynamic movement as signature of the system of metabolism and movement. When muscle is tensed isometrically, astral organization activity is congested and may awaken into awareness of pain when cramp develops.

With flowing movement on the other hand the intervention of the astral organization is dynamic. Both types of movement show further characteristic phenomena. Thus isometric contraction involves increased thrombocyte adhesiveness and a relative increase in LDL cholesterol. There is a tendency to consolidate which accompanies the dammed-up movement and a profile showing disposition for arteriosclerosis. The limited ability to relax (reduction in arterial compliance) has also been described (Miyachi/Kawano/Sugarwara/Takahashi/Hayashi/Yamazaki/Tabata/Tanaka 2004).[151] Conversely flowing movement is accompanied by a relative increase in HDL cholesterol and overall is more anti-atherogenic in its effects. Will-governed warming movement can also effect an improvement in the endothelial dysfunction (Hambrecht 2000).[152]

Setting the inner task

Apart from changes in lifestyle, medical treatment, eurythmy therapy and also art therapy, there is the field of the inner work that needs to be done by the patient. Terms like dealing with stress, etc. only point to this in a superficial way. It is the I's active contribution to therapy which can help to gain something from the illness and so achieve actual healing. How may we characterize this inner work that needs to be done?

The inner life of human beings has two polar opposite aspects—excess of form, rigidity (sclerosis) and overweening dynamics (dissolution). Both need to be guided by the individual spirit.

The two extremes have one thing in common. Life in the psyche has dropped out of the inner guidance of the individual, in the one case due to the tendency of the psyche to go rigid, in the other because the psyche's own dynamics are overweening. The I is not sufficiently in control of the psyche. The biography often shows a narrowing, with hamster-wheel-like busyness in a life that is full of stress. There is need to find moments of inner peace in the rush and haste of everyday life. This does not mean using external means to achieve relaxation or apparent calm, for there is passivity behind this and hence the individual is not actively present. Peace gained through inner activity of the I or self is needed. The ability to seek out an inner place of peace and quiet, with the soul at peace, can be acquired, helping to gain peace in the midst of outer hustle and bustle.

The 'six qualities' (Steiner 1989)[153] prove an important instrument for practice. Modern people are exposed to a flood of information and stimulation in their thinking and sensory perceptions. Vast numbers of impressions are gained through the many media, and people are unable to deal with it all, to digest it in independent thinking. The pole of conscious awareness irrupts into the inner life of people in the way described, generating illness. This is countered by developing active thinking, with powers of concentration, not looking only for distraction, and the ability to enter into contemplation and meditation (Trenkwalder 2000).[154] Arterial hypertension may involve cognitive problems and even dementia. Exercises of this kind can therefore also be preventive or help to improve symptoms.

The unfolding of the will has been subject to similar limitations. Western civilization has changed a life full of movement into one that is increasingly indolent where unfolding the outer will is concerned, lacking in movement. Human activity is progressively reduced to a mouse click and machines bring things that have been triggered in this way to realization. So there is less and less human activity in our society, as machines have taken over.

In the face of this we must develop and encourage the one sphere of human activity that will never be automated. All activities that are truly human, like comforting the sick in a loving way, or also giving personal encouragement, cannot be taken over by machines but demand that we are truly human. Apart from this challenge of our age there is the individual task of practising the unfolding of the will in the face of a progressively more retrograde human mobility which then turns into restlessness and states of excitement. This may be done with physical exercise in its different qualities. And there are also many exercises for training the will, among them the one which progresses from resolution to done deed, one of the six qualities, playing a central role.

Another major field where work needs to be done is that of feeling. Here the individual spirit must become the inner leader in one's feelings which will again and again escape the I's control because of the shock-like experience which has been mentioned or the inner fear and nervousness that cannot be overcome. The term 'job strain hypertension' relates to this dimension in the psyche. It is, above all, necessary to counter the stress which tells us that the dynamics of the psyche are predominantly governed from outside and seemingly no longer under the control of the I. The challenge is to be present in the individual spirit in everything one does, which is presence of mind in the real sense, rather than having one's mind already on the next but one point in the day's agenda. This also means practising patience, being able to wait for something and not rush towards the future. In his *Knowledge of the Higher Worlds* (Steiner 1993),[155] Rudolf Steiner wrote of the absolutely outstanding significance of patience. Without it, it is not possible to move forward in one's development.

The next step is to practise positivity. It is crucial to be able to see prospects and develop a justifiable mood of inner hopefulness. Profound trust in destiny, which the individual spirit has helped to shape, can develop. There is also another aspect to the positivity exercise in connection with arterial hypertension. People's minds are often troubled and full of care and they are not so much living in the immediate present with this but in a future full of care. Those worries may present a future that is negative in all its possibilities and blinds people to the way things are at the moment and the first signs of times to come. For people with high blood pressure it is a tremendous challenge to grow aware of what is truly positive, opening their eyes by letting go of the anxieties and cares that live in the psyche.

The fifth quality that needs to be practised is lack of bias, openness. Inner unrest and tension, in short, the element frequently experienced as stress, limit the way we see the outside world, for we are then living much more in our own world of thoughts and feelings. Because of this we fail to perceive many of the things around us, with our attention caught up in ourselves, taking ourselves too seriously as we concentrate on our inner life. Where the psyche is concerned, a mental world develops that is closed up upon itself, perhaps not even noticing that someone we pass is greeting us. Every mental gesture that is limited and in this sense head-like goes hand in hand with sclerosis and hardening at the physical level. Openness and an interest in others can develop into healing powers in this respect. This openness, interest and willingness to learn when we come upon things that are new and unknown arise from inner activity of the I.

These five exercises and the sixth which endeavours to bring the other five into harmony, letting them become habit, can do much to support medical treatment. The endangered human middle, where the mind pole of the nervous organization overstimulates or the soul dynamics of the metabolic system irrupt (increased by emotive experiences), is strengthened by doing them.

Major depression (unipolar disorders)

Wolfgang Rissmann[156]

Main idea

Depression is one of the commonest diseases of our time and most frequently the reason for early retirement. It is on the increase in western civilization, pointing to the inner problems and needs of modern people who have to depend on themselves, yet also offers the possibility of gaining a new orientation. Depression is more than a passing sadness. Melancholia reigns in the depths of the soul. Interest in the world fades, feelings turn grey, empty and joyless. Drive is also affected. Any kind of activity seems difficult and is ultimately not taken up. Those affected describe their condition as being like an inner prison from which there is no escape. The connection with the rest of the world is about to be broken, impressions of that world no longer reach the inner soul which no longer responds to external stimuli. Healthy self-confidence is put in question. Thoughts of personal guilt and shame concerning life so far gain tormenting certainty. Patients see their existence in doubt and long for the relief of peace and quiet; they are longing for death. During and above all after the depression there may also be signs of a longing to deepen life and give one's inner values a new orientation.

Symptoms and evolution

The main symptoms are depressed mood, joylessness and lack of interest, lack of drive and marked fatiguability.

Additional symptoms are reduced concentration and attentiveness, reduced self-esteem and self-confidence, feelings of guilt, shame and being of no value, negative, pessimistic outlook, suicidal thoughts, intended suicide and plans to commit suicide, sleep disorders (in both going to sleep and sleeping through the night), reduced appetite.

Other signs and symptoms which point to depression are general physical exhaustion and tiredness, pressure over the stomach, constipation, diarrhoea, weight loss, diffuse headache, sensation of pressure in throat and chest, sensation of lump in throat, functional cardiac and circulatory disorders such as tachycardia, arrhythmia, syncope, respiratory problems such as dyspnoea, vertigo, scintillating scotoma, visual disorders, muscle tension, diffuse neuralgiform pain, loss of libido, stopped periods, impotence, memory problems.

Depressive symptoms can be concurrent with many other physical and mental diseases.

According to ICD-10, distinction is made between four types. A somatic syndrome may be present in addition during mild and medium severe episodes and is always present with severe episodes. An episode of greater or lesser severity is considered recurrent if there is a history of at least one other. 15–20% of the populations of western civilized countries suffer from depression at some time or other, with women affected more frequently than men. The condition is developing earlier and earlier. One third of cases become chronic and will then frequently lead to early retirement. 60–70% of patients have suicidal thoughts during a depressive episode. 4% of all patients admitted to hospital once with depressive disorder and no particular suicidal element do later commit suicide.

Psychotherapy

Basic psychotherapy covers the following aspects: establishing a good relationship, active support by conveying hope, clarification of existing motivations and expectations of the therapy, conveying understanding of symptoms, that they can be treated, and the prognosis (psycho-education); clarifying any problem situations, reducing excessive demands, support in formulating definite wishes and achievable goals, including family, addressing suicidal impulses.

Psychotherapy broadened through anthroposophy is based on these general measures and will also deal with spiritual issues, biographic aspects, questions of meaning and destiny, also suggesting special exercises for the soul (attentiveness, mindfulness, etc.).

Psychotropic drugs

The five most important substances are tri- and tetracyclic antidepressants, SSRIs, selective serotonin-norepinephrine reuptake inhibitors, selective norepinephrine reuptake inhibitors, MAOIs.

Other categories of substances are also used, as are non-classified drugs like lithium, trazodone, buproprion, St John's wort.

Onset of action is generally in the second and third week of treatment. If there is no response after 3 weeks, increase the dose, consider changing to another drug or adding a second one.

See also official guidelines and the specialist literature.

Medical treatment and external applications

The various causes of depressive conditions are considered, as are their evolution, constitutional and typological aspects. The main focus is on the individual situation of patients.

With mild and medium severe forms of depression anthroposophic medicines and external applications used in addition to psychotherapy and art therapy will give lasting results. Severe depression usually calls for the exhibition of antidepressants in addition. In complex conditions that threaten to become chronic, anthroposophic medicines and above all external applications can stimulate marked relief and improvement.

Please note. The use of sulphur in any form requires medical supervision.

Distinctly neurasthenic constitution

Medical treatment

To vitalize generally and resolve hardening tendencies in the psyche:

- *Argentum met. praep. D6 trit.*/Weleda, 1 coffee-spoonful 3 times a day for 4 weeks.

To warm through and stimulate metabolism:

- *Sulphur D6 pilules*/Wala, 10 pilules 3 times a day for 1–4 weeks.
- Duration of treatment depends on responses such as increased restlessness, sweats, tendency to develop a fever.

To stimulate appetite and digestion:

- *Gentiana lutea e radice 5% pilules*/Wala, 10 pilules 3 times a day for 4 weeks, then change.
- *Abrotanum D1 dil.*/Weleda, 10 drops 3 times a day for 4 weeks, then change.

- *Herba Abrotani* tea/1 cup daily in the mornings for 4 weeks, then change to another tea, e.g. *Artemisia Absinthium, Teucrium scorodonia, Cichorium intybus.*

External applications

To warm through and stimulate light metabolism:

- Oil dispersion bath with *Eucalyptus Oleum aethereum 10%* /Wala, full bath once/wk for max. of 10 baths.

If seriously exhausted in addition:

- Bath with decoction of *Radix Calami*/full bath once or twice a wk for max. of 10 baths.

For cold feet and problems going to sleep:

- Footbaths with sulphur (*Kalium sulfuratum*)/daily at night for max. 4 weeks.

If not sufficiently warm and no history of pyrexia:

- Full baths with sulphur (*Kalium sulfuratum*)/once a wk for max. of 10 baths.
- *Hyperthermic Schlenz baths*, applied by trained staff in hospital environment, once a wk for up to 10 baths.

Distinctly hysterical constitution

Medical treatment

If boundaries against sensory impressions and emotional experience are inadequate:

- *Plumbum silicicum D6 trit.*/Weleda, 1 coffee-spoonful 1–3 times a day for 4–8 weeks.

If Plumbum silicicum does not elicit adequate response:

- *Plumbum met. praep. D6 trit.*/Weleda, 1 coffee-spoonful 1–3 times a day for 4–8 weeks.

It has to be noted, however, that individuals with sensitive psychic constitution may be more depressed when on Plumbum met. praep.

If psyche lacks structure and boundaries, also for dissociative and mild psychotic symptoms:

- *Stibium met. praep. D6 trit.*/Weleda, 1 coffee-spoonful 3 times a day for up to 3 months, in severe and acute states by s.c. or i.v. injection.

On the same indication if *Stibium* action is not strong enough:

- *Antimonit D6 trit., amp.*/Weleda, 1 coffee-spoonful 3 times a day for up to 3 months in severe and acute states by s.c. or i.v. injection.

Long-term basic treatment if skin and upper human being are not fully structured:

- *Quartz D10 trit.*/Weleda, 1 coffee-spoonful 3 times a day for up to 6 months.

For signs of an overweening fluid organism and tendency to hayfever, for tendency to develop dissociative symptoms:

- *Gencydo 1%, 3%, 5% amp.*/Weleda, s.c. in calves or between shoulder blades once a wk, or in severe cases 3 times a wk, changing concentration acc. to sensitivity and severity.

For anxious restlessness and problems going to sleep:

- *Bryophyllum 50% trit. or D1 dil.*/Weleda, 1 coffee-spoonful or 10 drops 3 times a day for 4–8 weeks.

To stimulate appetite and digestion:

- *Absinthium D1 dil.*/Weleda, 10 drops 3 times a day.

For severe hysterical states with poor appetite, flatus, tendency to diarrhoea:

- *Radix Gentianae*, aqueous cold extract/a sip hourly for 4 weeks.

External applications
For cold feet and problems going to sleep:

- *Powdered mustard footbath*/daily at night for 4 weeks, then change.
- *Lavender footbath*/Weleda, daily at night for 4 weeks, then change.

Disorder of lung process

Medical treatment

Marked emphasis on formal, abstract thinking with no mood changes, anankastic personality structure:

- *Pulmo Gl organ potency series, serial pack I amp.*/Wala, s.c. 3 times a wk for 4 weeks, 4 weeks' pause, then repeat if required.
- *Cinis Tabaci D6 and D20 amp.*/Weleda, D6 s.c. 3 times a wk for 4 weeks, then D20 for 4 weeks.

Frozen inner state with no feeling for rhythm, problems with making changes:

- *Mercurius vivus naturalis D12 trit.*/Weleda, 1 coffee-spoonful 3 times a day for 4 weeks, then change.

Nervousness, weak drive:

- *Ferrum sidereum D20 trit.*/Weleda, 1 coffee-spoonful morning and midday for 4–8 weeks.
- *Urtica dioica Ferro culta Rh D3 dil. or amp.*/Weleda, 10 drops 3 times a day or s.c. 3 times a wk for 4 weeks, then change.

External applications

- Chest compress with ginger/3 times a wk for 4 weeks, 2 weeks' pause, repeat if required.

Disorder of liver function

Medical treatment

For depression with functional epigastric symptoms such as pressure, sensation of fullness, tendency to be constipated, daily variation with morning low:

- *Cichorium D1 dil. or amp.*/Weleda, 3 times 10 drops or s.c. 3 times a wk for 4–8 weeks.

For acute depression with loss of vitality, adynamic state, tendency to dry up:

- *Taraxacum Stanno cultum Rh D3 dil. or amp.*/Weleda, 3 times 10 drops or s.c. 3 times a wk for 4 weeks.

For persistent depression tending to become chronic, dry, stagnating or overweening constitution, daily variation with morning low:

- *Stannum met. praep. D8 trit. or amp.*/Weleda, 1 coffee-spoonful 3 times a day or s.c. 3 times a wk for 3 months.

For acute depression with biliary stasis, inflammatory irritation of bile ducts, nausea in the morning, bad taste in the mouth, headache in conjunction with constipation, pain syndrome in right side of body, burning pain and pruritus of skin:

- *Chelidonium D1 or D3 dil. or amp.*/Weleda, 3 times 10 drops or s.c. 3 times a wk for 4–8 weeks.
- *Choleodoron dil.*/Weleda, 10 drops 3 times a day for 4–8 weeks.

For depression caused by toxic liver damage from alcohol, drugs and medicinal drugs:

- *Carduus marianus capsules*/Weleda, 1 capsule mornings and evenings for 3 months.

For general weakness, irritability, aggravation from cold temperatures, back pain and weakness in sacral region, weak heart and oedema:

- *Kalium carbonicum D6 dil.*/Weleda, 10 drops 3 times a day for 4–8 weeks.

For problems sleeping through the night, waking at about 3 a.m. and daily variation with morning low, tendency to be constipated, intolerance of fats:

- *Hepatodoron tablets*/Weleda, 3 tablets at night for 3–6 months.

External applications
For lack of drive, exhaustion, epigastric symptoms, intolerance of fats, daily variation with morning low:

- *Moist and hot compresses on the liver with added yarrow tea*/daily or 3 times a wk for 4 weeks, repeat after two weeks' break if required, then pause.

Similar to the above but mainly for gastric and digestive weakness:

- *Moist and hot compresses on the liver with added wormwood tea*/daily or 3 times a wk for 4 weeks.

For tendency to colicky pain in epigastrium and after traumatic experiences:

- *Moist and warm compresses on the liver with added Oxalis essence 10%*/Weleda, daily or 3 times a wk for 4 weeks.
- *Ointment patch on liver with Oxalis ointment 10%*/ Weleda, 1 hour daily for 4 weeks.

For marked lack of drive but with no inner unrest and risk of suicide:

- Ointment patch on liver with *Ferrum met. praep. 0.4% ungt.*/Weleda, for 30 min 3 times a wk for 4 weeks.
- Organ einreibung (special rhythmic medicated rub) of liver—as alternative to ointment patches with the indicated ointments 2 or 3 times a wk for a total of 4 weeks.

Disorder of kidney function

Medical treatment

For acute depression with inner frostiness, tension, restlessness, anxieties:

- *Melissa Cupro culta Rh D3 dil., amp.*/Weleda, 10 drops 3 times a day or s.c. 3 times a wk for 4–8 weeks.

For acute and subacute depression with inner emptiness, tension, restlessness:

- *Cuprum met. praep. D6 trit., amp.*/Weleda, 1 coffee-spoonful 3 times a day or s.c. 3 times a wk for 4–8 weeks.

For anxiety and panic states connected with depressive mood:

- *Cuprum met. praep. D20 trit.*/Weleda, 1 coffee-spoonful at night for 4–8 weeks.

For tension and restlessness, esp. in conjunction with hyper function of thyroid:

- *Chalkosin D4 trit.*/Weleda, 1 coffee-spoonful 3 times a day for 4–8 weeks.

Tendency to meteorism and spasms in intestinal region:

- *Carbo Betulae cum Methano D6 trit.*/Weleda, 1 coffee-spoonful 3 times a day for 4 weeks.

For severe dyspnoea, anxious nervousness and restlessness:

- *Carbo Betulae D20 trit.*/Weleda, 1 coffee-spoonful 3 times a day for 4–8 weeks.

Tendency to discrete fluid retention in eyelids, ankles:

- *Equisetum arvense Rh D6 dil., amp.*/Weleda, 10 drops 3 times a day or s.c. 3 times a wk for 4–8 weeks.

External applications

- Moist and hot compresses with *Equisetum arvense* on kidney/3 times a wk or daily for 4 weeks, repeat after 2 weeks if required, then pause.
- Tea with *Equisetum arvense*/1 cup in the mornings for 4 weeks.

To warm through if restless:

- Tea with ginger/1 cup in the mornings for 4 weeks.
- Moist and warm compresses with ginger on kidneys/3 times a wk or daily for 4 weeks, repeat after 2 weeks if required, then pause.
- Ointment patch with *Cuprum met. praep. 0.4%*/ Weleda, for 1 hour daily or 3 times a wk for 4–8 weeks.

Disorder of cardiac function

Medical treatment

Depression with dark mood, suicidal tendency, guilt feelings,

- *Hypericum Auro cultum Rh D3 dil., amp.*/Weleda, 10 drops 3 times a day or s.c. 3 times a wk for 4–8 weeks.

For depressive mood and guilt feelings, pangs of conscience, Da Costa syndrome:

- *Aurum met. praep. D20 trit., amp.*/Weleda, 1 coffee-spoonful once a day or s.c. 3 times a wk for 4–8 weeks.

For old people with beginnings of heart failure, shortness of breath and anxieties:

- *Crataegus drops*/Weleda, 10–20 drops 3 times a day for 4–12 weeks.

For Da Costa syndrome connected with anginal symptoms:

- *Cactus comp. II pilules*/Wala, 10 pilules 3 times a day for 4–12 weeks.

External applications
Depressive problems with going to sleep, turning things over in one's mind, cardiac symptoms, oppression:

- Ointment patches on the heart with *Aurum/ Lavandula comp. ungt.*/Weleda, daily at night for 4–8 weeks.

Inner chilliness, feeling unprotected in depressive moods:

- Oil dispersion baths with *Melissa ex herba W 5%, Oleum*/Wala, once or twice a wk for 4–8 weeks.

Chronic depression, esp. of older people
Medical treatment

The measures given can complement conventional treatment.
Persistent depressive mood, with resignation and guilt feelings:

- *Aurum met. praep. D20 or D30 amp.*/Weleda, s.c. 3 times a wk for 3 months.

Anxious nervousness, reduced vitality and weak drives:

- *Ferrum sidereum D20 trit.*/Weleda, 1 coffee-spoonful mornings and midday for 3 months.

Persistent depression with inner rigidity:

- *Mercurius auratus D15 amp.*/Weleda, s.c. 3 times a wk for 3 months.
- *Formica D30 amp.*/Weleda, s.c. once a wk for 3 months.

Seriously chronic with no warmth reaction, low basal temperature:

- *Iscucin Crataegi amp.*/Wala, s.c. twice a wk.

External applications
Seriously chronic with no warmth reaction, low basal temperature:

- Oil dispersion bath with *Viscum Mali ex herba W 5%, Oleum*/Wala, once a wk for up to 10 baths.
- Hyperthermic *Schlenz baths,* only given by trained staff in hospital context, up to 10 baths.

Painful experiences and shocks as triggers

Medical treatment

The following initial treatment is recommended:

- *Argentum met. praep. D6 trit.*/Weleda, 1 coffee-spoonful at night, always combined with *Oxalis* ointment patch.
- *Cuprum met. praep. D6 trit.*/Weleda, 1 coffee-spoonful at night for up to 3 months.

This treatment and psychotherapeutic conversation can be given to begin with for mild and medium severe depressive episodes, followed by the actual medical treatment for depression. Other depression-resolving medicines will be indicated at later stages; see above.

External applications

- *Oxalis 30% ungt.*/Weleda, apply to central epigastrium at night, initially for 4 weeks, pause for 4 weeks, repeat if required.

Severe mental and physical exhaustion, burnout syndrome as trigger

Medical treatment

Psychotherapeutic conversation, art therapy, eurythmy therapy and exercises (e.g. exercises for the soul), and:

- *Argentit D6 trit.*/Weleda, 1 coffee-spoonful at night for 4–8 weeks.
- *Cardiodoron dil.*/Weleda, 10 drops 3 times a day long-term.
- *Aqua Maris D3/Prunus spinosa Summitates D5 aa amp.*/Weleda, s.c. 3 times a wk for 4 weeks.
- *Levico D1 dil.*/Weleda, 10 drops 3 times a day for 4–8 weeks.
- *Hepar-Magnesium D4 amp.*/Weleda, s.c. 3 times a wk for 4–8 weeks.
- *Ferrum sidereum D20 trit.*/Weleda, 1 coffee-spoonful morning and midday for 4 weeks.
- *Neurodoron tablets*/Weleda, 2 tablets twice a day, morning and night.

External applications

- *Equisetum arvense essence*/Weleda, night-time foot-baths for 4 weeks.
- *Radix Calami tea*/full bath twice a wk for max. of 10 baths.

- *Lavender Bath Milk*/Weleda, full baths twice a wk for max. of 10 baths.
- Oil dispersion bath with *Prunus spinosa e floribus W 5%, Oleum*/Wala, full bath once a wk for max. of 10 baths.

Anthroposophic art therapy and eurythmy therapy

Treatment is complemented with various art therapies and eurythmy therapy. The art therapy process brings pleasure in being creative and self-confidence.

Therapeutic clay modelling stimulates delimitation from the outside world and powers of configuration in three dimensions. Painting therapy challenges sentience as colours are experienced. Music therapy and creative speech stimulate breathing and rhythm. Eurythmy and eurythmy therapy directly activate will and drive and encourage powers of sentience.

Otitis media

Georg Soldner[157]

Main idea

It is generally the case with inflammatory conditions that the organism seeks to deal with a particular organ or organ sphere by increasing metabolic activity—often supported by pyrexia—to make it its own again. Acute otitis media of children and adults may in the majority of cases be treated without recourse to antibiotics.[158] It is important to make the diagnosis quickly, exclude other serious inflammatory conditions in the respiratory tract, above all mastoid involvement in young children. Antibiotics are more likely to be advisable if otitis media and severe bronchitis occur together. The signs and symptoms of otitis media are subject to long-term fluctuations, and the incidence of mastoiditis has increased again also with conventional treatment; above all persistent effusions develop (mucoserous otitis), partly following relatively bland evolution of otitis media. A tendency towards chronic conditions, with 'cool' evolution may be also observed in this field. This is another reason for not using suppression initially but primarily strengthening the organism so that it will achieve proper ventilation of the middle ear again of its own accord. It is also advisable to avoid exposure to much noise for two or three weeks once the inflammation has gone down (this also means nurseries—up to 85 dB have been registered in conventional nurseries). Salutogenically it is of value to encourage the patients—mostly children—in active listening by approaching them with real interest.

General treatment

Parenteral treatment

It is often evident that starting treatment with a single (!) injection of *Silicea comp. amp.*/Wala, 0.3-0.5 ml s.c. over the mastoid on the affected side gives a much more reliable and better result. Using a short, fine needle (26G, $^1/_2$"), the injection is not really painful and easily controlled. As the inflammation tends to extend to the other side as well or may start bilaterally, it is advisable, in case of doubt, to apply treatment to both sides.

External applications

For as long as there is pain:

- *Aconite ear drops*/Wala, 1 or 2 drops into the meatus 3–6 times a day (at body temperature) are effective. If there is an effusion in the middle ear, always follow with

- *Levisticum H10% oil*/Weleda (a few drops of the oil on cotton wool introduced into the meatus), or
- *Levisticum ear drops*/Wala, 2 drops 2 or 3 times in the meatus; continue until middle ear is repneumatized.

If feet are cold and warmth organization is weak, a warm, rising-temperature (up to 40 °C) footbath (if indicated with the addition of 3 heaped tbsp of black mustard) relieves pain and supports the warmth organization, thus increasing the efficacy of the medicines listed below.

Acute inflammation

- *Levisticum Rh* (= non-alcoholic aqueous solution) *D3 dil.*/Weleda, 5–7 drops hourly or more frequently.

Combination with *Apis mellifica* has also proved effective; in low potencies it enhances the detumescent *Levisticum* action.

- *Apis/Levisticum II pilules*/Wala, 5 pilules hourly or more frequent.

The treatment is complemented with

- *Silicea comp. pilules*/Wala, 7–10 pilules 3 times a day.

Tendency to purulent type of otitis media:

- *Echinaecea Mercurius comp. suppositories*/Wala (under 7 years of age: *Echinaecea/Mercurius comp. suppositories for children*/Wala), 1 suppository once or twice a day.

For teething infants and young children (this is the age when the condition is most common) and if pain is severe:

- *Chamomilla comp. suppositories*/Weleda.

The nose should always be treated as well, not with detumescent nose drops but with *Nasenbalsam* (nose balm)/Wala (under 4 years of age, *Nasenbalsam fuer Kinder* (for children)/

Wala, 3 times a day, later once or twice a day, introduce well up into nose, or

- *Schnupfencreme* (nasal catarrh cream)/Weleda, use in the same way.
- *Rhinodoron Nasal Spray*/Weleda.

Diet. Temporary avoidance of milk (as far as possible), total avoidance of sweet things of any kind, and avoidance of rich dishes is advisable.

OME (glue ear)

In the case of glue ear or otitis media with effusion (OME), treatment of the acute symptoms needs to be continued until the ventilation problem has abated. Levisticum continues to be the most important medicinal plant also at this stage. If the condition persists for more than 14 days, the following would be suitable:

- *Levisticum, ethanol. decoctum D10 dil.*/Weleda
- *Mercurius solubilis Hahnemanni D12 dil.*/Weleda
- *Sylvin* (= sylvite, a natural potassium chloride) D6 dil./Weleda aa and 60 ml dil., 5–10 drops 3 times a day.

Other elements may be added to the mixture, as symptoms suggest.

It is important to continue with regular care of the nose and to support the warmth organism (e.g. with regular warm footbaths) (see also section on Rhinitis).

Persistent ventilation problem

Considering that many public nurseries have noise levels of up to 85 dB, and that on the other hand the tensions in families are almost unbearable for both children and parents, etc., we realize the wide variety of things that are intolerable. It is important to give thought to this issue and provide relief. A ventilation disorder may develop when the individual concerned can't (and won't) bear to 'hear' something.

Potentized gold—used for about 6 weeks—provides support for many patients under mental strain who develop ventilation problems in their ears.

- *Aurum metallicum praeparatum D12 trit.*/Weleda, a heaped coffee-spoonful every morning.

External applications in home nursing

Adults and especially children can both benefit and suffer harm from all forms of sensory impressions. External applications therefore play an important role in the family medicine chest. Some examples will serve to illustrate this. It is important that the applications are made calmly and with loving concentration. Careful attention and devotion to the task are part of the complex therapeutic process. The examples given below also prove to be useful home nursing measures. They were developed by the author together with Petra Lange, mother of five children, when working on *A Waldorf Guide to Children's Health: Illnesses, Symptoms, Treatments and Therapies.*[159,160] At the right temperature substances penetrate deeply through the skin, reaching all organs in their regions and functions. Thus it is possible to ease breathing, loosen mucus, regulate body temperature and reduce pain. Beneficial sensory experiences and a feeling of being safe and secure develop at the same time.

Chamomile compress on the ear

- for mild earache
- follow-up treatment of otitis media.

Wrap a handful of dried chamomile flowers in a thin cotton fabric. Knead briefly so that if will fit more snugly over the ear and heat by putting it between two plates placed on a pan of boiling water like a lid. This is the best way of retaining the essential oils without the compress getting wet. Thoroughly warmed through, the compress is placed on the ear, covered with an intermediate wool or silk cloth (unspun raw wool or cotton wool if not available) and tied in place with a woollen scarf or hat.

Duration: at least 30 minutes or overnight.

For follow-up for up to 14 days overnight.

Chamomile compresses have a pleasant scent and are very popular with children. They must be renewed when the scent fades (after 4 or 5 treatments).

Onion compress for the ear

- for severe earache.

Finely chop a medium-sized onion and tie up in thin fabric to make a roll the thickness of a finger. Place behind and on the ear at body temperature, cover with wool or silk (unspun raw wool or cotton wool if not available) and use a woollen scarf or hat to keep securely in place.

Duration: 30 minutes.

Lemon juice throat compress, hot

- for mild sore throat, also for hoarse teachers.

Put half an untreated lemon, preferably biodynamic or organic in a small towel and cover with very hot water. Make several cuts in it and express (using a fork to hold it and a beaker to express the juice). If the lemon has been treated use only the juice, diluted with hot water.

Fold fabric that is not too thin or cut to size so that it fully covers the throat but not the region of the vertebral column.

Roll the fabric up from both sides to the centre, place in a somewhat larger wringing-out cloth and immerse, keeping the corners dry.

Pick up the wringing-out cloth by its corners, wind around the tap and wring out firmly. The dryer the hot compress is the better will it be tolerated on the skin.

Take the compress out of the wringing-out cloth, place around the throat, starting from the larynx, as hot as is bearable and as smoothly as possible. Use a woollen scarf to hold in place.

Duration: at least 5–10 minutes.

Chest rub with essential oils

With oil of lavender, eucalyptus or mountain pine, 10% max.

- Alternative to chest compress with essential oils.
- A rub calls for calm, concentrated movements of warm (!) hands and a small amount (!) of oil.
- Apply rub to the whole chest, using the indicated oil, then cover with a woollen cloth.

Ointment cloth over the heart

With *Aurum/Lavandula comp. cream*

- for nervous, anxious children with (going to) sleep disorders.
- Apply ointment thinly to a pre-warmed patch of bourette silk or cotton and place over the heart when going to sleep.
- Vest will as a rule keep it in place.
- If warmth is needed, wrap a silk scarf or woollen cloth around the chest.

Duration: overnight.

Abdominal compress with yarrow

- Make the tea with ½ litre boiling water poured over a handful of yarrow, cover and leave to draw for a good 10 minutes.

- Roll up a cloth of suitable size from both sides to the middle and place on a larger cloth to make wringing out easier.
- Pour the tea on this through a sieve.
- Wring out firmly, remove compress and place on abdomen as hot as possible.
- Tie a woollen scarf large enough to go round the body smoothly around to hold compress in place. The scarf should go well beyond the compress so that no areas of cold develop.
- Put two hot water bottles, not filled too full, over the abdomen from either side so that their tops meet over the middle of the abdomen.

Duration: 30–60 minutes, then loosen the scarf slightly and pull out the compress.

Leave the scarf in place for the rest period (1 hour) or overnight.

Bladder compress
With *Eucalyptus oil 10%*

- For urinary infections.
- Soak a piece of bourrette silk or cotton fabric the size of the palm of your hand in the oil and warm well.
- Place over the bladder region and secure with a woollen fabric or a layer of unspun raw wool.
- Keep in place with close-fitting underwear.

Duration: Once a day for several hours, until cured, and if indicated also for 1 or 2 weeks longer.

Calf compress

- To reduce a temperature.

These compresses must not be applied if feet and/or legs are cold, even with high temperatures! When feet and legs are still cool, the body needs a great deal more support for the intended warming effect to ease the development of a temperature. However, if the legs feel hot on touch, one can start to reduce the temperature and relieve the circulation.

In preparation, put a thick cotton fabric (e.g. a bath towel) on the bed to protect the mattress.

- Put 2 or 3 litres of water in a bowl, its temperature barely lower than the measured body temperature.
- The action is intensified by using lemon water. Put half an untreated lemon, preferably biodynamic, in the water, make a number of cuts in it, and express firmly against the eminence of the hand. If the lemon has been treated, put two tablespoonsful of the juice in the water.

  Vinegar made from fruit juices may be used instead.

- Roll up two towels or cloths reaching from ankle to below the knee and large enough to go one and a half times around the leg and dip them in the water.
- Wring them out so that they will not drip, then apply.
- Wrap each leg in turn from ankle to knee, securing the cloth with a large woollen stocking, a woollen scarf or a thick cotton cloth. Do not use watertight fabrics or plastic!
- Keep the child covered during the treatment, with just a light blanket or sheet if the temperature is high. The wrapped-up legs must also be under cover.

Cloths will have grown warm in 5–10 minutes and need to be renewed.

Pause for half an hour after three changes.

Stop the treatment if the feet grow cold.

Calf compresses at body temperature are a reliable treatment to reduce a temperature. Parents will usually need to give it at night. Here are some useful tips that have proved effective:

- Have not two but four towels/cloths ready. You will then have a fresh set ready when changing.
- Pull out the warm cloth, open up the woollen outer cloth and immediately put a fresh cloth around the leg, which will still be a bit damp.

Linen fabric has proved particularly helpful for calf compresses. They are a bit firmer when damp than when they are dry and do not give the feeling of constriction one gets when cotton fabrics dry up.

Mustard footbath

- For inflammation in nasal, nasal sinus and pharyngeal region, polyps, enlarged tonsils.
- Possibly also incipient migraine.

Tie up one or two handfuls of freshly ground mustard powder in a thin cloth and put, tied ends down, in a bucket containing water at 37–39°C.

Duration: up to 10 minutes. Avoid the footbath cooling down by placing a bath towel across the knees.

The mustard bath must not be in touch with mucous membranes. Rinse the legs after the footbath.

The skin will turn very red, although this may only happen after several footbaths.

As a rule apply only one footbath a day.

To conclude the treatment, apply a gentle vegetable oil such as mallow oil, lavender oil 5% or olive oil to the legs.

Ginger and salt footbath
People with sensitive skin will often tolerate ginger and salt better than mustard footbaths.

- Briefly bring 2 tablespoons of ground ginger to the boil in about ½ litre of water. If tolerance is good, the quantity may be increased up to 4 tablespoons. Freshly expressed ginger juice may be used instead.

- Prepare a really warm footbath with a handful of added sea salt and add the ginger paste (or juice).

Duration: about 10 minutes (if burning sensation, stop sooner).

Rinse feet with lukewarm water and apply sage oil (*Oleum salvia 10%*) or olive oil.

Cool compresses

- Dilute 1 tablespoon of the essence with 9 tablespoons of water.
- Dip a fairly thick cloth (e.g. double layer of bourrette silk) in the liquid. Wring out so that it will not drip and place smoothly, without creasess, on the area to be treated.
- Secure with a woollen scarf or a thick cotton cloth.
- Use a ladle or small jug to pour some of the diluted essence into the compress at intervals to keep the inner cloth moist.

with Arnica essence

- For contusions, muscle strain, sprains
- Change at least once a day. Do not use if Arnica allergy or open skin wound.

with Calendula essence

- For abrasions, weeping wounds.
- Change hourly, using freshly ironed inner cloths or sterile gauze compresses.
- After some hours allow the uncovered wound to dry.

Tip. This compress allows adherent dressings to come off without pain.

Compress with low-fat curd cheese (quark)
for galactostasis

- In case of mastitis only if monitored by physician or midwife.
- For sunburn, contusions, muscle strain, sprains.
- The size of the cloth depends on the size of the area to be treated.
- In case of sunburn, contusions, muscle strain, sprains, apply a cool compress.
- Leave nipple free when applying the compress.

In case of galactostasis or mastitis remove the compress about 20 minutes before the next feed. Gentle application of oil to the breast stimulates milk flow and also warms the breast.

Caution. Not suitable for people allergic to cow's milk and a tendency to develop eczema.

Diet

In anthroposophic medicine, diet focuses on constituents, composition and palatability as well as some other aspects. These are helpful in providing a healthy diet in sickness and in health. We find them by considering the human constitution.

Food is always also transformation, change. All four levels of human existence are involved in this. The physical organization takes in nutrients. The I organization provides for their degradation with the help of digestive enzymes developed by the etheric organization. These are released into the whole digestive canal. Having passed the intestinal wall the nutrients are taken up into the blood in the portal vein which goes to the liver and enters into the vital system of the etheric organization. When the blood with those nutrients flows through the kidneys it enters into the sphere of the dynamic soul functions of this organ system—expansion and contraction, concentration and dilution. This gives the nutrients soul quality and takes them to the I organization. It adds warmth and the food thus becomes spiritual and can no longer be demonstrated physically. The heart plays a major role in taking nutrients into warmth. It is the organ in which, and by the activity of which, the metamorphosis of powers of growth into powers of thought takes place (see page 33ff). For fractions of a second the life-bearing blood comes to a halt at the end of every diastole before the next systole or

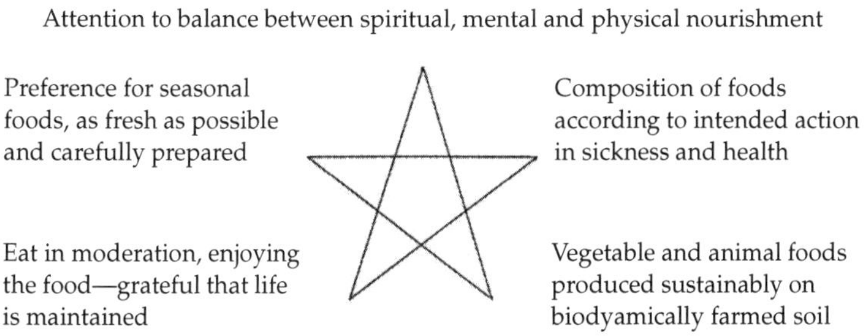
Attention to balance between spiritual, mental and physical nourishment
Preference for seasonal foods, as fresh as possible and carefully prepared
Composition of foods according to intended action in sickness and health
Eat in moderation, enjoying the food—grateful that life is maintained
Vegetable and animal foods produced sustainably on biodyamically farmed soil

The five principles of nutrition in anthroposophic medicine

contraction of heart muscle casts it into the great arteries, the aorta and the pulmonary trunk. That brief halt is like a minor death impulse for the etheric organism, with its circulating vitality brought to a sudden halt. That enables the etheric, astral and I organization to come free of its body-related functions and turn to life in soul and spirit. Rudolf Steiner wrote of this spiritual and physical physiology of nutrition in the first five chapters of *Extending Practical Medicine, Fundamental Principles Based on the Science of the Spirit*, recommending physicians to consider dietary aspects when treating any serious disease and so support a vitality that has been reduced in the morbid process.[161] A comprehensive work on the basics of this disease-orientated, detailed anthroposophic dietary treatment still needs to be written. There have, however, been significant pioneers such as Gerhard Schmidt, Udo Renzenbrink and Petra Kühne who have published books and papers on the essential aspects, different syndromes and the medicinal use of individual foods.[162,163,164]

A widely read introduction by Otto Wolff, doyen of anthroposophic medicine after the Second World War, bears the title *What are we really eating?* It is also worth reading the several volumes based on Friedrich Husemann's work *The Anthroposophic Approach to Medicine.*[165]

Diet maintains the physical structure of organs and organ systems in a steady state of balance, again and again effecting its complete renewal over the years. It means that the organizing systems of forces, which are active and give direction in body substance, retain their identity, whilst nutrients come and go. From childhood to old age the way in which our physical and spiritual nourishments relate to one another changes. In childhood the emphasis is on physical, in old age on spiritual nourishment. Food for the soul is equally important from the beginning to the end of life. Feelings of peace, of gratitude, love and trust—and especially also humility and veneration of the truth—are constructive and maintain life.

The figure on page 113 illustrates this dual process of spiritual and physical nutrition. No other symbol is better for demonstrating the functionality of the etheric organization than the open lemniscate. It is not just that it reflects the cardiovascular system, with the lemniscate representing the heart closed at the top but open to the great veins and arteries in which blood flows in and out. Its polar functional dynamics correspond to the equally polar functional dynamics of the ether organization, and the organization serving thought life show correspondingly opposite orientation.

The open lemniscate shows the polar opposite relationship between the body-developing, incarnating activity of the levels of existence and the activities taking effect outside the body, constituting conscious life in soul and spirit. When the body has too much to digest, that activity begins to fail. The consequences are tiredness and increased need for sleep. If the diet is not enough, with most of it easily digested, the consequences are increased wakefulness, nervousness and being 'a bit outside oneself'. This is often made worse by difficulties going to sleep and, in conjunction with this, a chronic sleep deficit. Regular and moderate meals provide for balance between physical and mental capacity appropriate to the given age. It is a lifelong task.

A manual for this way of nourishing soul and spirit at different ages, always in conjunction with the current physical nutrition, is also still outstanding. However, the relevant literature does offer various suggestions. It seems to me that, particularly in view of the future, it will be necessary to develop this relationship in a well-differentiated way. On the one hand a large proportion of humanity are overeating, and yet every ninth

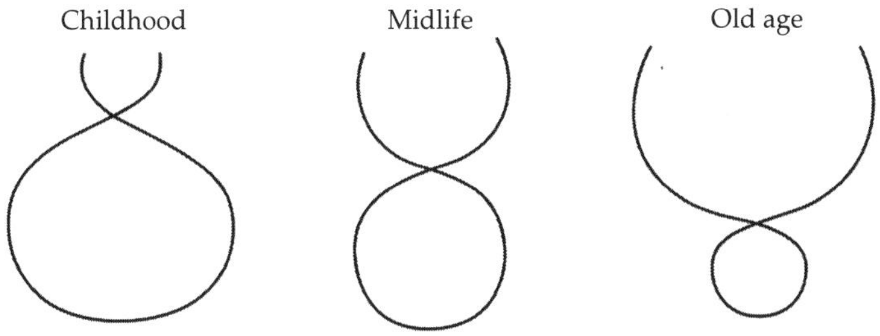

Physical development and involution

individual goes to bed hungry at night. Few can afford a diet that has biological value and has been sustainably grown. This calls for a change in awareness that can also include educational issues which help to provide insight into spiritual nourishment. 'Mankind shall not only live on bread but on every word that comes from the mouth of God.'[166] Spiritual and physical nourishment support one another. It is most important that more attention is paid to supporting the soil and the seed. We therefore have major initiatives in anthroposophic education for special needs and social therapy where biodynamic agriculture and seed researches are fully integrated, an example being the Bingenheim Community in Germany.[167]

Biography Work

Wisdom of my higher self,
holding your wings over me
And always my guide,
As would be best for me—
When vexation befell me—well,
It was a boy's vexation.
Now mature, the man's eyes
Have the power to rest on you in gratitude.
Christian Morgenstern[168]

It was not only in the context of Waldorf education that Rudolf Steiner gave detailed accounts of the laws governing the development of body, soul and spirit, and childhood and youth. It was important to him to expound on the laws of biographical development between birth and death when speaking of reincarnation and individual kinds of destiny configuration.[169,170]

On the basis of this, pioneers like Bernard Lievegoed and Gudrun Burkhard, and also the psychiatrist Rudolf Treichler, investigated these laws and made them accessible for everyday therapeutic use.[171,172] Compared to psychotherapy, biography work gives everyone who is interested the opportunity to find meaning in his or her own biography and be more consciously involved in shaping their future lives. This must be clearly distinguished from anthroposophic psychotherapy and psychosomatics, which require conventional study, as well as the study of anthroposophic psychotherapy, as qualified further training.[173]

Biography work is therefore a nonspecialized additional qualification which everyone can obtain whatever his professional field, broadening his or her area of competence. Used by physicians it uses a primarily therapeutic approach; a priest would integrate it into his or her pastoral care. Psychologists, social workers, art therapists, counsellors and business consultants will, on the other hand, offer it as part of their professional work.

The basis of training is to work out one's own biography and sensitization to biographic situations of others in connection with this. The role of the I or self as the centre and starting point of every biographical development is particularly important. To develop an interest in the wholly individual course of everyone's destiny is something that can only be achieved in dialogue with the client. It is, however, also possible to do one's own biography work for oneself by consulting works on the subject and finding one's way through one's own biography by taking counsel and being active on one's own behalf.[174]

The role and meaning of biography work is always to realize that life is a process of development and learn to say yes to it and enjoy it. It will then also be possible to look at one's relationships in a new light. Occasions will arise to appreciate the relationships in a new way, heal them and/or develop them further.

It often needs great inner strength for this, and objectivity and selflessness in identifying with a biography that does not please one and where one would never have wished or thought that it would have to be brought to realization. One may have had very bad experiences and would never wish others to have them, in fact never considering such things to be possible. One may have to work through experiences that struck at one's very core, causing damage. However, if one gives thought to the laws that govern repeated lives on earth one may also ask oneself: What does this tell me? Does it have to do with my personal destiny or am I here a child of my nation, of a specific age, so that it is the destiny of the nation or the age which is reflected in my personal biography, something I can bear and for which I can share responsibility? Yet when it is primarily my own concern I may ask myself: Would I be able to see that I, too, committed cruelties in an earlier life? Could you bear to accept that you were an evildoer? Could you bear it to realize that the individual with whom you have the greatest difficulties in this life is someone whom you may have harmed in an earlier life? To envisage oneself as the victim is much, much easier than to identify with the role of the perpetrator. Once one has lived with questions like these one can try to move on, asking oneself: What do I have in my present life that might balance out and heal possible unpleasant aspects of one of my earlier biographies?

People will spontaneously tend to reject unfavourable destiny elements, calling them unfair, and consider others to have been responsible. We are more inclined to take the good things that come to us as being justifiably ours.

When biography work also extends to this spiritual level it enters directly into personal development work, something which is so necessary today. We read about it, for instance, in Steiner's *How to Know Higher Worlds*. Suggested exercises provide the means to train faculties that will enable one to be oneself whatever destiny presents and see life itself as a way of development with the character of initiation. Such inner work, whichever way it is taken up to begin with, is of inestimable value in coping with the conflicts that arise in daily life. The very thought that life's events have something to tell us and could provide occasion to develop new faculties, can help us to feel more free and enterprising towards the way others behave towards us, and also to look at our own life more calmly and with equanimity. If we consider not only the past with its causes but above all the (positive) consequences for the future, we shall be motivated to do what we can to give events a positive turn and so help to create a positive future.

Anthroposophic Psychiatry and Psychotherapy

Anthroposophic psychiatry had its beginnings with the neurologist and psychiatrist Friedrich Husemann, MD. He established the Friedrich Husemann Clinic in Wiesneck near Freiburg in 1930. With its spiritual view of the human being anthroposophy offers a new starting point. It shows that it is the supersensible human being who develops the physical body, albeit unconsciously so. It is therefore possible to derive the psychopathological symptoms from the metamorphosis of the levels of human existence (see page 33), understanding their relationship to the organs, and treat them accordingly. (See the example given on page 85ff.)

From 1975 onwards a study and research group, one of the first initiative groups for psychotherapy in Germany and the Netherlands, started to create the conditions for the development of a specifically anthroposophic psychotherapy and its further training programmes in many countries. In 2012 Ad Dekkers, one of the representatives of this initiative, provided an important basic work entitled *A Psychology of Human Dignity*.[175]

Thanks to the anthroposophic scientist and physician Gunver Kienle a study of the placebo effect was available as early as 1995 which also attracted international attention. Her comprehensive investigation of the existing placebo literature as to which phenomena had been mistakenly attributed to the placebo effect, shows that so far there is no prospect of a scientific basis for the existence of the postulated placebo effect.[176]

The Placebo Effect

The existence of the placebo effect has been considered to be a scientific fact for more than 40 years, but Kienle was able to show the questionable nature of the data and assertions on the subject. Factors that may wrongly appear to be placebo effects are the therapeutic effect of a doctor-patient relationship that provides certainty and security, spontaneous recoveries, belief in the treatment, a strong desire to get well, a new, positive view of the disease, the beginning of an important human relationship, spontaneous fluctuations in health, adjuvant treatments, psychosomatic effects, psychotherapeutic effects and much more. Other factors that may wrongly suggest a placebo effect are the effects of selection, things said to please, conditioned information, uncritical use of anecdote, misquoting, wrong interpretation of everyday symptoms and much more. Conclusion: The phenomenon called the placebo effect is something with a definite effect that has not been identified or investigated. It will need to be investigated and given a proper scientific name rather than introducing the pseudo term placebo into science.

The processes which take effect in sickness and health are many-layered and this calls for a view of the human being where the functions of body, soul and spirit can be related to one another. It will then be possible to differentiate clearly between what is happening or has happened and the stopgap 'placebo'.

Art Therapies[177]

'Art is one way of grasping the I that is pulsing with life, tempered by life, but also carefully considered and filled with sun.' That is how Marie Steiner defined the central 'active mechanism' of all artistic work, including art therapies.[178] For art therapies have in common that they appeal to the creative I or self. This—the artist in us, the creative human being—is awakened, stimulated and becomes constructive, with the relevant positive effect on the relationship between body and soul.

The art therapies used in anthroposophic medicine have evolved partly from Waldorf education where artistic activity takes the form of a detailed age-specific, development-promoting curriculum and partly from therapeutic indications. On the other hand, Ita Wegman took this up at her Institute in Arlesheim and developed art therapy further also for use with sick and extremely sick people. A third point of origin was the involvement of some artists in the fields of speech, art and singing, music, painting and sculpture who wanted to serve people in ill-health. Thus anthroposophic art therapy has developed in differentiated ways at different schools in Australia, Belgium, Brazil, Finland, France, Germany, India, Italy, New Zealand, the Netherlands, Russia, Sweden, Switzerland, Slovakia, Spain, the Czech Republic and the United Kingdom. In some of those countries—for instance in Germany, Switzerland and the Netherlands—it has already become an integral part of health care provision.

Below are some aspects of the therapies which relate to the way we see the levels of human existence and indicate the direction of their therapeutic effects.

According to Rudolf Steiner in *Art as Seen in the Light of Mystery Wisdom*, work done in the arts originates in freely handled activities of those levels of human existence (see page 29ff.) The physical body maintains form and architecture.

The ether body has the power to be creative, to generate. The astral body is musical by nature. The I organization uses the laws that govern speech. In growth and development the levels of existence follow the natural laws of evolution. In art the same laws are handled freely, giving expression to man's creative powers. In this way, art reveals 'hidden laws of nature', as Goethe put it. These are the laws of the human soul and spirit, laws that have their roots in man's will to be free. With the help of these powers to configure things (not necessities of nature!) he can imitate natural and technological things, giving expression to personal experience, and also make supersensible elements, experiences and visions gained in the spirit, visible and perceptible to the senses. Depending on the medium used, the artistic abilities and laws present in different ways. But it is always the human I which uses the creative potential of the levels of existence.

Architecture therapy

The laws used in building the physical organization are imitated and freely combined in the art of architecture. Organic architecture also takes its form principles from those of skeletal structure, tendons and muscles with their inherent statics and dynamics. The shape of our bones and the functional use of arms, legs and the whole human figure may be seen in architectural columns. The rectangle which the arms can create, the cube, the dome of the head, the oval form of the trunk—all of them are projections of the physical constitution. Architecture is therapeutic when its proportions are in harmony and there is a clear geometrical composition behind it. Forms, and the way they relate to one another, are perceived through the senses and inwardly followed just as colours and sounds are, but less consciously so. Reactive depression connected with housing situations can disappear completely within a few weeks if the ceiling of the room is higher, colour and light come into play—even if the new flat has the same floor area as the old one.[179,180] In

Waldorf School buildings, Camphill establishments and clinics those beneficial effects provide the basis for an architecture therapy that still awaits further development.[181,182,183] Aspects of building biology also come into this, as does the way the environment is shaped.

Modelling therapy

In modelling, the visualizing, thinking activity of the etheric organization is brought together with the creative, configuring activity of arms and hands. For physical diseases this is utilized to strengthen the ether body.[184] Modelling capital and lower case letters is helpful in treating dyslexia in school-age children.

Behavioural problems of children and psychiatric conditions in young people and adults have been found to respond to the modelling of the five platonic solids, for instance, also for inpatients.[185] Generally, starting with a harmonious sphere, the 'middle' between the perfection of a thought in geometry and the readiness to act, i.e. as yet undefined, will function, if one proceeds calmly, step by step to create those new, pure forms. The individual comes to himself, breathes more deeply and gains distance from his everyday problems.

Painting therapy

In the book he wrote for painters, Leonardo da Vinci said that one could distinguish the inexperienced from the professional painter in that the former does not realize that in painting he presents and projects himself and his own way of experiencing the world. A professional painter knows what he is creating, and can distinguish projections from elements presented objectively using his painting skills.[186]

An anthroposophic therapist lets his patients paint freely in their own way during the first lesson. They will, of course, reveal something of their illness, projecting it onto the paper in colour and form. If the therapist is not sure of the diagnosis he lets the patient go on painting freely. Those early images are diagnostic. They provide inspiration for the therapeutic process using the means of painting therapy.

In accord with this, Rudolf Steiner advised Waldorf school teachers not to let children paint 'as their tums dictate'. Why? It may be meaningful now and then, so that the teacher can see the children's current state of health, but the aim of teaching is to set 'professional' tasks, exercises done individually to have a beneficial effect on the child's development. Painting addresses primarily the soul, bringing changes that have a positive, stimulating effect on the physical constitution.[187,188,189] Well-established indications for painting therapy are depression, rheumatic conditions, pain and helpful measures in palliative medicine for the quality of life of bed-bound patients.

Music therapy

The astral organization follows the laws of music. Here the I experiences itself in its die-and-be-born-again nature.[190] It is not surprising, therefore, that 'musical dialogue' in therapy touches on the most inward inner experiences. With music, people gain direct experience of their inner nature. Abysses, ascents and descents and the turbulences of life, but also self-awareness being torn apart and shattered into fragments. All these experiences, difficult or impossible to put into words, can be expressed directly as music with its rhythms, dissonances, abrupt pauses, tensions and harmonies. The therapeutic use of this proves helpful in treating a large number of syndromes.[191,192] Music therapy is particularly suitable for behavioural disorders in childhood and youth,[193] eating disorders, problems with concentration, lack of impulse control, addiction[194] and anxiety disorders. Scientific studies have now established that music therapy promotes intelligence and brings order into the development of the brain and nervous system, something which is now accepted in conventional medicine.[195]

Singing therapy

Sung vowels bring differentiation into the soul's experiences, inner deepening and also expression. As the sound vibrates through the human form, powers that have been dammed up and blocked can begin to flow again. Enlivened and harmonized by sound, singing therapy can thus help to find a new inner equilibrium.[196] Singing is also suitable for preventing depressive moods in melancholic children.

The anthroposophic singing therapist Valborg Werbeck-Svaerdstroem developed a new therapeutic method of singing and this has come to be called 'Uncovering the Voice'. Training and further training are currently available in Switzerland, Germany, Brazil and the USA.[197]

Therapeutic speech

With the word, a higher reality enters into the human soul. Speaking projects a wisdom that lies in the speech, in the word itself. Real entities, realities, are connected with words. We have many occasions to use the powers of the word for therapy: in the therapeutic dialogue, in meditations for the sick, with poems, prayers, and in working with the word itself.

Below are two examples of meditations for the sick. Speaking them quietly, gently, in a slow, clearly articulated way for oneself, one can immediately sense something of the power to bring order.[198]

> I think of my heart
> It gives me life
> And warmth
> I rely utterly
> On the eternal self
> Active in me
> That sustains me.[199]

> Peace within me,
> I bear within me

The powers that give strength.
I want to fulfil myself
With the warmth of these powers,
Filling myself
With the might of my will.
And I want to feel
How peace is pouring
Through all I am
When I gain strength.
Peace as power
I find in me
Thanks to the might of my endeavour.[200]

Speech therapists may also work directly with speech, as in conventional speech therapy. Rudolf and Marie Steiner have developed a plethora of articulation, vowel and breath-regulating exercises for this.[201,202,203]

Eurythmy therapy[204]

Eurythmy therapy developed from the eurythmy which came into existence as an art form between 1912 and 1924. Educational eurythmy was added in 1919 and eurythmy therapy from 1921 onwards.[205] Beatrix Hachtel produced a comprehensive bibliography listing not only papers published on the subject but also research findings that confirm its efficacy.[206,207]

In his eurythmy course[208] Rudolf Steiner noted that, 'Every form is a movement that has come to rest.' Eurythmy movements adapt the physical organization to the laws of movement and of flow in the etheric world, i.e. the creative movements that produce the human form. Erich Blechschmidt (1904–1992), human embryologist and anatomist, substantiated this by recording and publishing the embryo's movements in the course of its development (see page 26ff).

Today, ultrasound recordings with high resolution will also make the forms, functions and movements of the laws that govern eurythmy and the forms given to air in speech visible.[209]

The therapeutic effect of these movement processes may develop in four ways.

1. Inwardly going along with a eurythmic stage performance and imitating this through the senses.
2. In education, where the age-specific eurythmy curriculum at Waldorf schools encourages body and soul to mature from kindergarten to upper school.
3. In hygienic eurythmy with generally stimulating or consolidating exercises vocalizing and/or emphasizing the consonants of verses or poems and with tone eurythmy exercises. The effect is regulative, centring and harmonizing. These exercises are particularly effective if done in a group. This adds the cheerful, humorous or also quiet and serious but always positive qualities of human relationships.
4. In eurythmy therapy as such, where the gestures used in eurythmy as a performance art and in education are modified so 'that they flow from the morbid nature of the individual just as the others do from a healthy constitution'.[210] Here the orientation given to the power of the sounds or a specific movement is such that it can direct its positive action towards the diseased organ or organ system.

Examples of eurythmy figures

Movement – yellow
Feeling – red
Character – blue

All four principles are based on the specific healing quality of eurythmy, which is that the physical body takes up the flow forms and creative impulses of the etheric organization more intensely and this allows them to act in a stronger and more specific way.

The movement of the sound addresses the form aspect which is performed by the human form as a whole and gives the movement its meaning, its expression in body language. This form and meaning aspect is reflected in the eurythmy figure's garment. The feeling motion belonging to the sound gesture is shown in the colour of the veil. However, the muscle tension which gives the movement its character is the will aspect of the sound and thus the third colour mood. Body and soul in their totality are therefore required to adapt to the regenerative creative impulses of the etheric.

Anthroposophic Nursing With Physical Contact and Effort[211]

In 2007 a German health insurance company for engineers responded to a questionnaire concerning patients' satisfaction by putting the anthroposophic Havelhoehe Community Hospital in Berlin first among the 200 German clinics included. Other polls that followed gave equally good results. As a rule anthroposophic hospitals have above average good results for patient satisfaction because anthroposophic nursing is outstandingly good. It is taught at government-approved nursing colleges and has brought a new culture into nursing as a profession.

Depending on the severity of the condition, nursing is the crucial third element between physician and patient. Attitude and gesture, conveying the offer of help to someone who is helpless in such a way, creating such an atmosphere that the sick individual will be happy to accept nursing procedures to the very end—this is not self-evident. It has to be learned and applied to good effect. Nursing is repellent if there is no humanity, no dignity and spiritual orientation, and must be filled with genuine understanding of human nature. Otherwise it is in danger of being humiliating.[212]

Twelve gestures are characteristic in nursing. Depending on the given situation they need to be specially taken into account: To create a free space, to envelop, balancing out and harmonizing, stimulation, stressing, arousing, affirming, bringing upright, cleansing, nourishing, relieving and defending. These basic gestures guide our actions in anthroposophic nursing, the aim always being to help the individual concerned to be more independent again and have autonomy, or at least to an existence with greater human dignity.[213] When it comes to practical measures, anthroposophic nursing complements conventional nursing with measures such as compresses, packs and special medicated rubs.[214,215] Acute and chronic symptoms and disabilities will often not fully respond to medication. Here, it is nursing which improves the quality of life and can give people a feeling of being appreciated, having dignity, and arouse new courage to live. I shall never forget how a woman who had been an inpatient at the Herdecke/Ruhr Community Hospital for some time said, when she was discharged, that here she had regained her faith in the meaning of being human. One would very much hope that in future the nursing profession will also be given better recognition in financial terms.

Rhythmic massage and physical contact and effort

This covers various areas: work involving physical contact (massage), movement (gymnastics) and external applications, here especially hydrotherapy.[216]

Rhythmic massage and Simeon Pressel massage
Massage has an influence on the whole human being.

- Physically: Physical damage is properly and skilfully corrected or at least reduced.
- Vital energies: Vital processes are stimulated and, to a degree, also guided: breathing deepens, rhythmic processes may settle down at the functional level.
- Psyche: The patient feels accepted as he is; the atmosphere created permits, promotes and captures emotions.
- Mind and spirit: The patient finds himself respected as an individual. He is master of his disease and actively involved as a full partner in the therapy.

The relationship between patient and therapist is as close, as immediate and inward as with no other therapy. The step of crossing the boundary between the bodies of therapist and patient is minimal and absolutely crucial.

It is an art, and the responsibility of the therapist, to achieve the greatest possible degree of closeness and openness, at the same time preserving the patient's full integrity and dignity.

A bit of practical help is to uncover only the parts of the body to be treated at the time. This is taken into account with all forms of anthroposophic massage, with practical experience provided in training.

Currently, further training for nursing staff and contact therapists are Rhythmic Massage after Ita Wegman, MD, and Margarethe Hauschka, MD,[217,218] as well as massage after Simeon Pressel, MD.[219]

Hydrotherapy / baths

To date baths have taken the form of brushing, rising and falling wave and lemniscate baths. These were originally developed at the Institute of Clinical Medicine in Arlesheim led by Ita Wegman, MD.

The different rhythmic movement baths all have their specific indications (see Marbach 1991).

Friction or brush baths helps with circulatory disorders, sluggish metabolism and depression. They are in regular use in psychiatry because they activate the I organization by developing warmth, strengthening the I organization, especially in the case of depression or dissociative personality disorders.

The rising wave bath helps the process of inhalation, the falling wave bath influences exhalation and has a regulative effect on hypertension.

Lemniscate baths act on the warmth organism and circulation when treating rheumatic diseases affecting the joints. A special aspect of the last-mentioned baths is that the patient's body is not touched directly. Instead, hand movements are made above water that has been set in motion so that they reach the patient in rhythmic sequence. Water does have the power to circulate rhythmically and here is the therapeutic instrument, sometimes complemented with oils or therapeutic bath products.

The patient first rests for a little while in the water which envelops the body. Then the therapist's hands reach into the water, uniting with this element and beginning to set the water in motion with specific hand movements. The hands may, for instance, start from the head region and move downwards on both sides of the body. Previously at rest, the water is slightly held back by the moving hands, evading them by moving sideways and creating vortices that run behind. At the body's boundary, the patient's skin, the moving water takes effect by exerting slight pressure, finally flowing away, a rippling echo. The wave is reflected just a little on the skin boundary but does, at the same time, generate an inward-moving impulse, moving the fluid organism in the body. The circular movements made beside the joints during lemniscate baths create additional warmth.

Water responds to the subtlest nuances of movement. It calls for a high degree of attentiveness to give configured impulses. Every repetition takes a different course. Therapists—and the patient—are removed from the everyday ways of thinking and acting with their more or less mechanical focus. During the rest that follows there can be a genuine 'coming to' and sense of well-being. One returns to the daily round feeling stronger than before.

Werner Junge developed the oil dispersion bath in 1937. From about 1960 it has been used as a treatment. The international association for oil dispersion bath therapy maintains a website where full information is given.[220]

Bothmer Gymnastics and Spacial Dynamics

In anthroposophic medicine, movement therapy is based on a holistic view of the human being as a life form that is physical, alive and at the same time has soul and spirit. It does not only benefit the organism but harmonizes the person as a whole.

Movements flow in time, both in the circulation of body fluids and in all forms of deliberate movements at work and in play, facial expression and gestures, speech, gymnastics and physical exercise.

Deliberate movements have a goal, serving to concentrate and firm. The movement patterns and qualities lead to tension, contraction to the degree of hardening, but also to self-perception, even through pain. The same applies to everyday movements of which we only grow aware through pain when we realize that our movement forms have become one-sided. Even minor changes, consciously made in posture when standing and sitting, walking and reaching, can result in major changes.

On the other hand, movements arising from the powers of will are spontaneous and unconscious. The will's action in the organism leads to expansion, radiation, rounding out. The predominant character of movement is flowing, dissolving and going out far and wide. The inner experience of this is one of joy and lightness, vaguely connected with the world, as if at one.

Between conscious awareness and will lies the feeling aspect of the soul's experience. Here, the processes of movement impulses governed by thought and sensory perception meet and interpenetrate, leading to centering and concentration with intentional movements that radiate out. So if an imbalance has arisen this is the best point from where regulation may come. Balance between the contracting processes of conscious awareness and the radiating processes of activity creates the free space for creative, artistic endeavours.

The brain mass floats calmly, protected, in the cerebrospinal fluid. The metabolic organs, on the other hand, are in constant motion. Respiration and blood circulation mediate in tireless, lifelong rhythm between movement and rest, between inner and outside world. The gymnastics are mainly using the will element. The desire to move is involved. Without the appeal to the life of feeling, without joy and the psyche being involved, the movement would seem soul-less, uninvolved, mechanical and compulsive, i.e. not truly human. Yet when the will is reached by activating the life of feeling, many possibilities arise to regulate the total composition of the organism hygienically and therapeutically.

Currently there are two forms of training and further training in anthroposophic movement therapy. On the one hand, the gymnastic exercises that Fritz Count von Bothmer developed in collaboration with Rudolf Steiner especially for the Waldorf School curriculum.[221] The other is the movement training and therapy developed by Jaimen McMillan/USA (Spacial Dynamics). This was originally based on Bothmer Gymnastics but has its own approach to movement.[222] Metamorphosed into therapy and adapted to the indicated syndromes, both approaches and types of exercises serve anthroposophic movement therapy. This includes eurythmy therapy, which imitates the movements of etheric development, the Bothmer exercises, which derive from the laws of the physical body, and the Spacial Dynamics exercises where the intention comes more from the astral side of the inner life.

Education for Special Needs And Social Therapy[223]

Apart from her clinic in Arlesheim, Ita Wegman, the first anthroposophic physician and from 1924 onwards leader of the Medical Section at the Goetheanum, also established the first institute for special needs education in Arlesheim/ Switzerland. This was the Sonnenhof. Rudolf Steiner then gave twelve lectures on special education from 25 June to 7 July 1924 at the Goetheanum. A number of children from the Sonnenhof were presented at those lectures. Rudolf Steiner explained the therapeutic prospects to the physicians and special needs teachers who attended.[224,225] Based on those lectures anthroposophic education for special needs and social therapy spread worldwide, getting known particularly as the Camphill movement. This was initiated in Scotland by the Austrian physician Karl Koenig (1902–1966), a Jewish immigrant and friend of Ita Wegman. A special way of life was developed where carer and those in need of care lived and worked together in relatively large establishments, usually embedded in a village setting with biodynamic agriculture, school, workshops and the sale of products.

Thanks to Ruediger Grimm we have an extensive bibliography for this specialist field.[226] For many years the head of the anthroposophic movement in special education within the Medical Section at the Goetheanum (www.khsdornach.org) and professor of special needs education at Alanus University Alfter, with the focus on theories and methods in the field, he made a major contribution to anthroposophic special needs education in a constructive dialogue with academic special and special needs education.

The keynote with anthroposophic work in special needs education is the conviction that the core of man's being, the individual spirit, can never be sick but only impeded or impaired in the development of body and soul. The work does not take the impairment and the limitations and impossibilities connected with it for its starting point but rather orientation in the essential nature and individual potential of the individual concerned. This is a challenge for both carers and those in care. Professional competence is one part of this, the humour one needs day by day and qualities such as a sense of responsibility, conscientiousness, powers of empathy, interest and courage are the other essential parts.

Reflection on one's own actions and attitude, study of the anthroposophic view of the human being and the will to understand and respect every individual with his peculiarities and bias in the context of his destiny are the preconditions for a diagnosis and treatment that will be the basis for our actions as we work together in eurythmy therapy and medicine. Another key element is to create an environment in which development and fulfilment will be possible. Too much is very often asked of people with disabilities in our hectic present age, isolating them. Because of this, time processes are carefully configured in anthroposophic institutions, especially concerning the course of the day, week and year. This can create a therapeutic atmosphere, an environment that offers external and inner support, making people feel certain and sure, increasing their confidence and trust in themselves and the world.

Regular artistic activities and experience in eurythmy, painting, music, speech, modelling and handwork are of outstanding importance. For the artistic element is often the only bridge that will allow those concerned to get in touch with their body and also with the given social environment.

The basic rights—life, education and work—apply to all people. Even when financial means are getting scarcer there must not be regulations that limit or discriminate against people with disabilities but only society providing support in solidarity.[227,228,229]

The UNESCO decision to give the same human rights to people with disabilities as to others who are not in need of special support has therefore been epoch-making. The reasons given are as follows:

> In recognition of the valuable contribution that people with disabilities can and do make to the general welfare and diversity of their communities, and the recognition that the promotion of the full enjoyment of human rights and fundamental freedoms by people with disabilities and their full participation in them increases the feeling of belonging and leads to considerable progress in society's human, social and economic development and the overcoming of poverty. So-called people with special needs or disabled people make a significant contribution to the humanization of mankind.[230]

To take note of this and make it bear fruit in social life was and has been the aim of anthroposophic education for special needs and social therapy ever since they were established and also for the concept of inclusion that has arisen from this.[231]

Research In Anthroposophic Medicine

The list of currently available anthroposophic medicines was developed by physicians and pharmacists or manufacturers working together. The ideas for new medicines always came from concrete questions arising in the work with patients or their medical conditions. The basic research consisted in establishing correspondences between morbid processes in human beings and specific processes in the natural world or specific effects of substances. It is a matter of finding and describing natural processes that stimulate self-healing in the given situation, counteracting functions that have grown too powerful or too weak for supporting them. The more accurately the therapeutic aim can be defined by investigating the evolutive relationship between man and nature, the more certain will, as a rule, be the desired effect for the patient. The safety and effectiveness of the raw materials are generally well known, so that there is no preclinical research such as in-vitro and animal testing. The usual criteria to establish safety apply when new natural substances, for which no monographs exist, are used. An anthroposophic medicine is expected to ameliorate physical or mental symptoms and contribute to a cure, or to prevent a disease. Identification of the indicated medicine and its use are generally geared to the individual patient and it needs methods of research and evaluation that are in accord with this.

In July 2000 Helmut Kiene, Freiburg physician and scientist, published a complementary methodology for the established clinical research, postulating cognition-based as distinct from evidence-based medicine.[232] The method of single-case analysis developed for this extends to the evidence areas of proof of efficacy, effectivity assessment and comparison with other methods of treatment. In 2003 his institute[233] also published a comprehensive monograph on mistletoe in oncology.[234] This is the first publication which makes the present status of mistletoe therapy in oncology available to the medical profession, scientists and people who take a general interest. It contributes not only to the scientific discussion of important medical principles but also to the dialogue concerning styles of thinking. Anthroposophic cancer and mistletoe research has since progressed—the prospective pancreatic cancer study, most recently presented, showed not only improved quality of life but also a significant extension of life.[235]

At the research centre at the Havelhoehe Community Hospital in Berlin the aim of a project designed to evaluate anthroposophic medicine was to establish a scientific data basis as a foundation for demonstrating safety and efficacy of anthroposophic medicines in everyday practice. Using networks supported by information technology, outcome and provision research are thus developed further within anthroposophic medicine.[236] In the School of Medicine at Witten-Herdecke University, a chair for theory of medicine and complementary medicine was established under Prof. Dr Peter Matthiessen. Apart from research and teaching this also involves the implementation of a part-time course in anthroposophic medicine. In Bern/Switzerland, KIKOM (Kollegiale Instanz für Komplementaermedizin) was established at the request of local citizens in 2003. Swiss physician Peter Heusser[237], MD, was required to lecture in anthroposophic medicine, with colleagues doing the same for homoeopathy, herbal medicine and traditional Chinese medicine. He succeeded Prof. Matthiessen at Witten-Herdecke in 2009, with Dr Ursula Wolf taking over his position in Bern. The chair at Witten-Herdecke University has now been taken over by Prof. David Martin, its designation changed in 2009 to Chair for Theory of Medicine, Integrative and Anthroposophic Medicine. At the Hogeschool Leiden in the Netherlands, Prof. Eric Baars has occupied the chair for anthroposophic health care since 2007.

Outward evidence of experimental research must always be combined with the inner accord which is gained by taking the route of meditation. The philosophical quest for truth is not left aside in anthroposophic medicine but given central significance. Gerhard Kienle, private lecturer, co-founder of the anthroposophic hospital in Herdecke and the (not anthroposophic but method-pluralistic) private Witten-Herdecke University, has dedicated his scientific life to the quest for truth.[238,239]

Today there are more than 20 habilitated scientists in the clinical and research fields in anthroposophic medicine and a growing number of chairs and research institutes of complementary and integrative medicine, with anthroposophic medicine with its integrative medical system fitting into that context.[240]

This research culture is taken very seriously and is also the reason why acceptance of anthroposophic medicine has developed further in Germany, especially in recent decades. Thus a devastating review of anthroposophic medicine had, for instance, appeared in *Deutsches Aerzteblatt* (a major medical journal) in the early 1990s, but in 2004 the same journal published an item the title of which read 'Conventional and complementary medicine—need to gain deeper insight and increase collaboration'. This change in attitude was partly due to growing demand for complementary medicine and partly to the demonstrable good practical experience in anthroposophic hospitals, as well as the outcome of an initiative established as Dialogue Forum for Pluralism in Medicine in 2000. That had been suggested by Prof. Joerg-Dietrich Hoppe (1940–2011), president of the Federal Medical Council in Germany in collaboration with health economist Peter Meister, former manager of the anthroposophic hospital in Herdecke, Matthias Girke, MD, at the time head of the Havelhoehe anthroposophic hospital in Berlin and from October 2016 head of the Medical Section at the Goetheanum, Prof. Peter Matthiessen, now emeritus professor of theory development in medicine at Witten-Herdecke University, Prof. Guenter Ollenschlaeger, head of the medical centre for quality in medicine in Berlin, Prof. Hermann Heimpel, formerly medical director of the medical unit at Ulm University Hospital, Helmut Kiene, MD, head of the institute of applied epistemology and medical methodology in Freiburg, and

Prof. Stefan Willich, head of the Institute of Social Medicine at the Charité in Berlin.[241]

What is more, anthroposophic medicine was from 1980 to 1992 represented at the largest European congress for further education in medicine held in Berlin, above all thanks to the personal initiative of the late Lore Degeller, MD, a prominent anthroposophic physician, and Prof. Gotthard Schettler, for many years the congress president and at the time occupying the chair for medicine, medical director of the university hospital in Heidelberg and president of the Heidelberg academy of sciences for the promotion of holistic medicine.

As a result of this and an initiative of women patients, the first German scientific congress for integrative breast cancer treatment was held under the patronage of Dr Frank-Ulrich Montgomery, president of the Federal Medical Council, the German society for haematology and oncology and the patients' representative in the Federal Government. Dr Harald Matthes' talk on the approach used in anthroposophic medicine attracted much attention and was a step along the road, so that today the Berlin-Havelhoehe anthroposophic hospital is recognized throughout Germany as a centre for the treatment of breast cancer. From 1980 oncology has become one of the most interdisciplinary and integrative medical research fields and that is not least due to the wide-spread and effective use of anthroposophic mistletoe therapy with Iscador®/Helixor, abnobaVISCUM®abnoba, Iscucin®/Wala and Isorel®/LUKAS Heilbetriebsstaette.

Anthroposophic medicine is also represented at the major international congress for integrative medicine. From 2008 onwards it is on the scientific committee, the programme committee, in workshops, symposia, with plenary lectures and posters at the Congress for Integrative Medicine/ECIM that is held in different places. At the 6th ECIM congress, held in Berlin in 2013, with Harald Matthes co-president, a broad spectrum of current clinical research findings was also presented that came from the anthroposophic research centres—in integrative oncology and anthroposophic mistletoe therapy, pain management, chronic inflammatory bowel diseases, cardiology, neurology/ psychiatry, Whole Medical System research, consensus-based CAse REporting (CARE), guidelines development, therapeutic use of Rhythmic Massage and therapeutic speech, doctor-patient relationship and problems connected with values.

In 1997 the Medical Section at the Goetheanum collaborated with Prof. Robert Gorter in a first congress for academic research in anthroposophic medicine. This impulse was taken further in collaboration with KIKOM (Kollegiale Instanz für Komplementaermedizin) at Bern University in 1998, the Havelhoehe research centre in Berlin in 2012 and at the University for Applied Sciences in Leiden/Anthroposophic Health Care Dept. in 2014. On each occasion, the current status of anthroposophic medical research was presented to and discussed with the internal and external public. It was particularly at the congresses in 2012 and 2014 that experts in anthroposophic medicine were able to enter into dialogue with renowned representatives of conventional medicine. 'CAM—Complementary and Alternative Medicine. The challenges of scientific research in Finland' was a milestone in the Far North where integrative and complementary medicine has not yet really found its feet. That was at Tampere University on 13 November 2015. The coordinator was the anthroposophic gynaecologist Peter Zimmermann, M.D.

Another milestone was the '1st International Congress for Integrative Health and Medicine. A conference combining the presence of anthroposophic medicine, integrative medicine and functional medicine' in Stuttgart in June 2016. This was convened by the Academy of Integrative Health & Medicine (USA) and the umbrella organization for anthroposophic medicine in Germany (DAMiD) together with the major umbrella organizations of integrative medicine in the USA and Europe for methods, concepts, experience, perspectives and research findings in integrative medicine especially in the fields of oncology, paediatrics and cardiology.[242] The following declaration was adopted by the 600 congress members from 40 countries:

We call on governments:

- To recognize integrative health and medicine as a whole society approach that will help to reach the Sustainable Development Goals;
- To include integrative T&CM into national health service delivery and self-care, as agreed in the WHO Traditional Medicine Strategy 2014-2023 and several World Health Assembly resolutions;
- To collaborate with integrative health and medicine research centers, practitioners and civil society in establishing integrative health and medicine policies;
- To create and fund ambitious public research programs to increase evidence of T&CM treatments and integrative care models;
- To establish and support systems for qualification, accreditation or licensing of integrative medicine practitioners;
- To adopt medicine regulation pathways tailored to the specific nature of traditional and complementary medicines.

We call on the World Health Organization:

- To prioritize the implementation of the WHO Traditional Medicine Strategy 2014-2023;
- To adopt, whenever relevant, an integrative health and medicine approach across WHO departments and strategies to reach the Sustainable Development Goals;
- To facilitate regional collaboration of countries and to closely collaborate with T&CM research centres, practitioners and civil society to advance the implementation of the WHO Traditional Medicine Strategy.

We call on professional organizations:

- To actively support the implementation of WHO Traditional Medicine Strategy, including through certification of T&CM practitioners and practices.

Notes

[The umlaut (¨) is the letter e. Ä, Ö, Ü, ä, ö, ü may therefore also be written Ae, Oe, Ue, ae, oe, ue]

1. Steiner R., Meuss A., *Physiology and Healing*, CW 311. Forest Row: Rudolf Steiner Press.
2. Glöckler M., Girke M., Matthes H., Anthosoposophische Medizin und ihr integratives Paradigma. In Rahel Uhlenhoff (ed.) *Anthroposophie in Geschichte und Gegenwart*. Berliner Wissenschaftsverlag, Berlin 2011.
3. Heusser P., *Anthroposophische Medizin und Wissenschaft: Beiträge zu einer ganzheitlichen medizinischen Anthropologie*. Schattauer Verlag, Stuttgart 2010.
4. See also http://www.anthromed.de.
5. Steiner R., Wegman I., Meuss A., *Extending Practical Medicine. Fundamental Principles based on the Science of the Spirit*. CW 27. London: Rudolf Steiner Press 1996.
6. Steiner R., Barton M., *Illness and Therapy. Spiritual-Scienific Aspects of Healing*. Forest Row: Rudolf Steiner Press.
7. Glöckler M. (ed.) *Anthroposophische Arzneitherapie für Ärzte und Apotheker*. 5. Folgelieferung. Wissenschaftliche Verlagsgesellschaft Stuttgart, Stuttgart 2014. [Publication of English translation in progress]
8. Girke M., *Innere Medizin. Grundlagen und therapeutische Konzepte der Anthroposophischen Medizin*. Salumed Verlag, Berlin 2012.
9. Soldner G., Stellmann H., Michael K., *Individuelle Pädiatrie*. Wissenschaftliche Verlagsgesellschaft Stuttgart, Stuttgart 2011.
10. Glöckler M., Goebel W., Michael K., *Kindersprechstunde—Ein medizinisch-pädagogischer Ratgeber*. Verlag Urachhaus, Stuttgart 2015.
11. Evans S S., Repasky E A., Fisher D T., Fever and the thermal regulation of immunity: the immune system feels the heat. *Nature Reviews Immunology* 15:335-349, 2015.
12. See e.g. Fröhlich-Gildhoff K., Rönnau-Böse M., *Resilienz*. Ernst Reinhardt Verlag, München 2015.
13. Bonhoeffer D., *Widerstand und Ergebung. Briefe und Aufzeichnungen aus der Haft*. Dietrich Bonhoeffer Werke, 8. Band. Gütersloher Verlagshaus, Gütersloh 2011.

14. Wolfram E. Paracelsus., *Die okkulten Ursachen der Krankheiten: Volumen Paramirum*. Nach d. Aufl. 1912, Verlag am Goetheanum, Dornach 1991.
15. Daems W.F., *Streifzüge durch die Medizin- und Pharmageschichte*. Verlag am Goetheanum, Dornach 2001.
16. Steiner R., Lindemann W., CW 2., *The Science of Knowing*. Spring Valley: Mercury Press 1988.
17. Steiner R., Lindemann W., *Truth and Science*. CW 3. Mercury Press 1993.
18. Steiner R., Stebbing R., *The Philosophy of Spiritual Activity*. CW 4. Rudolf Steiner Press. Other translations entitled *The Philosophy of Freedom*.
19. See also https://www.goetheanum.org.
20. CW 4. See Note 18.
21. Steiner R., Bamford C., *How to Know Higher Worlds. A Modern Path of Initiation*. CW 10. Hudson: Anthroposophic Press 1994. Other translations entitled e.g. *Knowledge of the Higher Worlds*.
22. For further information see http://www.goethenum.org/Allgemeine-Anthroposophische-Gesellschaft.336.o.html.
23. Rosslenbroich B., *On the Origin of Autonomy. A New Look at the Major Transitions in Evolution*. Springer, Heidelberg, New York 2014.
24. See Rudolf Steiner Archiv, Dornach/Schweiz: http://www.rudolf-steiner.com/rudolf-steiner/biographie-2/.
25. Steiner R., *Schriften. Kritische Ausgabe (SKA)*. Band 7: Schriften zur Erkenntnisschulung. Herausgegeben und kommentiert von Christian Clement. Frommann-holzboog, Stuttgart, und Rudolf Steiner Verlag, Basel 2014, S. XLIII.
26. Peter Sloterdijk im Gespräch mit Mateo Kries. In *Die Welt*, 25 October 2011.
27. Steiner R., Creeger C E., *Introducing Anthroposophical Medicine*. CW 312. Dornach 1999.
28. Steiner R., Creeger C.E., *An Outline of Occult Science*. CW 13. A number of other translations.
29. Glöckler M., Einblicke in die anthroposophische-medizinische Forschung und die Arbeit der Medizinischen Sektion. In Christiane Haid, Constanza Kaliks, Seija Zimmermann (ed.) *Goetheanum—Freie Hochschule für Geisteswissenschaft. Geschichte und Forschung der Sektionen*. Verlag am Goetheanum, Dornach 2017.
30. Original in Morgenstern C., *Wir fanden einen Pfad*. Dornach: Rudolf Steiner Verlag 2004.

31. Steiner R., Kemmis B., *The Spirit of Fichte Present in Our Midst*. In CW 65. London: Rudolf Steiner Publishing Co., n.d.
32. Steiner R., *The Philosophy of Spiritual Activity / Freedom*. Various translations.
33. Steiner R., Lindeman W., *The Science of Knowing*. CW 2. Spring Valley: Mercury Press 1988. Also Steiner R., Wannamaker O.D., *The Theory of Knowledge Implicit in Goethe's World Conception*. New York & London: Anthroposophic Press and Rudolf Steiner Publishing Co. 1940.
34. Steiner R., *Selbsterkenntnis und Welterkenntnis vom Gesichtspunkte der Geisteswissenschaft*. Vortrag vom 23. April 1915. Dornach: Rudolf Steiner Verlag 1995.
35. Glöckler M., Grün A., *Kinder suchen Wahrheit: Spiritualität in der Erziehung*. Arlesheim: anthrosana 2008.
36. Glöckler M., *Wahrheit und Lebenskraft*. Esslingen: Gesundheitspflege initiativ, 2009.
37. Glöckler M., *Engelgestütztes Handeln—Liebe bewegt und heilt*. Esslingen: Gesundheitspflege initiativ 2010.
38. Steiner R., Adams G & M., *Anthroposophical Leading Thoughts*. CW 26. 1st Leading Thought. London: Rudolf Steiner Press 1973.
39. Arendt H., *Denken ohne Geländer. Texte und Briefe*. München: Piper Verlag 2006.
40. John Scotus Eriugena, *Periphyseon (The Division of Nature)*, tr. I. P. Sheldon-Williams and J J O'Meara, (Montreal: Bellarmin, 1987).
41. Morgenstern C., *Wir fanden einen Pfad*. Dornach: Rudolf Steiner Verlag 2004.
42. Hoerner W., *Zeit und Rhythmus: Die Ordnungsgesetze der Erde und des Menschen*. Stuttgart: Urachhaus Verlag 2006.
43. Steiner R., Adams G & M., *Occult Science. An Outline*. CW 13. London: Rudolf Steiner Press 1962/3. Other translations with same or similar title.
44. Ibid.
45. Sheldrake R., *The Presence of the Past: Morphic Resonance and the Habits of Nature*. London: Icon Books 2011.
46. Lima-de Faria A., *Evolution without Selection: Form and Function by Autoevolution*. Philadelphia/PA: Elsevier Science 1990.
47. Husemann F., Wolff O, Davisson L., *The Anthroposophic Approach to Medicine* Vol. I and II. Various editions.
48. Girke M., *Innere Medizin*. Berlin: Salumed Verlag [2]2012.
49. See also Steiner R., Wegman I., Meuss A R., *Extending Practical Medicine*. CW 27. Earlier translation entitled *Fundamentals of Therapy*.

50. See also Steiner R., *An Occult Physiology*. CW 128. Various editions.
51. See also Selg P., *Okkulte Physiologie: Rudolf Steiners Prager Kurs (1911)*. Arlesheim: Verlag des Ita Wegman Instituts 2015.
52. Claudius O., Baraff L J., Pediatric emergencies associated with fever. *Emergency Medicine Clinics of North America* 28:67–84, 2010.
53. Emde B., Tetzner H., Selbstmedikation. In Glöckler M (ed.), *Anthroposophische Arzneitherapie für Ärzte und Apotheker*. Wissenschaftliche Verlagsgesellschaft Stuttgart 2014.
54. Hamre H J., Glockmann A., Schwarz R., Riley D S., Baars E. W., Kiene H., Kienle G. S., Antibiotic Use in Children with Acute Respiratory or Ear Infections: Prospective Observational Comparison of Anthroposophic and Conventional Treatment under Routine Primary Care Conditions. *Evidence-Based Complementary and Alternative Medicine* 2014: http://dx.doi.org/10.1155/2014/243801.
55. zur Linden W., *Geburt und Kindheit*. Frankfurt: V. Klostermann Verlag 1992, S. 337–350.
56. Glöckler M., Goebel W., Michael K., Creeger C., *A Waldorf Guide to Children's Health: Illnesses, Symptoms, Treatments and Therapies*. Floris Books 2018.
57. Soldner G., Stellmann H M., *Individuelle Diagnostik und Beratung*. Wissenschaftliche Verlagsgesellschaft Stuttgart. Stuttgart 2011, S. 83 ff.
58. For full details of damage caused by vitamin D, see Seelig M S. Vitamin D and cardiovascular, renal and brain damage in infancy and childhood. *Ann. New York Acad. Sci.* 1969, 147: 539–582.
59. As Note 49.
60. Schmitz H., *Kurze Einführung in die Neue Phänomenologie*. Verlag Karl Albert, Freiburg i. Br. 2014.
61. Vgl. Eggert, J W. Das biopsychosoziale Krankheitsmodell. Grundzüge eines wissenschaftlich begründeten ganzheitlichen Verständnisses von Krankheit. *Psychologische Medizin* 2: 3–12, 2005.
62. Glöckler M., Girke M., Matthes H., Anthroposophische Medizin und ihr integratives Paradigma. *Anthroposophie in Geschichte und Gegenwart*. Berliner Wissenschafts-Verlag, Berlin 2011.
63. Steiner R., *Von Seelenrätseln*. Part translated as *The Case for Anthroposophy* by O. Barfield. London: Rudolf Steiner Press 1970.
64. Aus Blechschmidt E., *Die vorgeburtlichen Entwicklungsstadien des Menschen*. Atlas. Karger 1995.
65. As Note 63.

66. Schad W., *Säugetiere und Mensch. Zur Gestaltbiologie vom Gesichtspunkt der Dreigliederung*. Verlag Freies Geistesleben, Stuttgart 1985.
67. Steiner R. As Note 63.
68. Schiller F., Wilkinson E M., Willoughby L A., *On the Aesthetic Education of Man*. Clarendon Press 1967.
69. Schiller F., *The Death of Wallenstein*. Gutenberg Project.
70. See *Beiträge zur Rudolf Steiner Gesamtausgabe, Nr. 34*. Rudolf Steiner Verlag, Dornach 1971, S. 23.
71. Steiner R., Everett R., *Soul Economy and Waldorf Education*. CW 303. New York & London: Anthroposophic Press and Rudolf Steiner Press 1986.
72. See Glöckler M., Langhammer S., Wiechert C (ed.). *Gesundheit durch Erziehung*. Förderstiftung Anthroposophische Medizin, Dornach 2006.
73. See Glöckler M (ed.). *Das Schulkind—gemeinsame Aufgaben von Arzt und Lehrer*. Verlag am Goetheanum, Dornach 1998.
74. See Glöckler M (ed.). *Gesundheit und Schule. Schulärztliche Tätigkeit an Waldorf- und Rudolf Steiner Schulen*. Verlag am Goetheanum, Dornach 1998.ü
75. See for instance Alexander E., *Proof of Heaven. A Neurosurgeon's Journey into the Afterlife*. Piatkus 2012.
76. Van Lommel P., *Consciousness Beyond Life: The Science of the Near-Death Experience.* Harper One 2011.
77. Ibid.
78. See Note 76.
79. Steiner R., Wegman I., Meuss A.R., *Extending Practical Medicine*. CW 27. London: Rudolf Steiner Press 1996.
80. See also Internationale Gesellschaft für Anthroposopische Tiermedizin (IGAT) unter Http://www.ggtm.de/tierhalter/therapien/anthroposophische-tiermedizin/.
81. Spranger J., *Lehrbuch der anthroposophischen Tiermedizin*. Sonntag Verlag, Stuttgart 2007.
82. Greenpeace. *Europe's Pesticide Addiction*. Free download under https://www.greenpeace.de/sites/www.greenpeace.de/files/publications
83. Kipp F A., translator not named. *Childhood and Human Evolution*. Adonis Press 2005.
84. Rosslenbroich B., *On the Origin of Autonomy*. Springer Verlag, Berlin/New York 2014.

85. See Note 79.
86. Hirte M. Impfen: *Pro & Contra—Das Handbuch für die individuelle Impfentscheidung*. Knaur Mens-Sana. München 2008.
87. Goebel W., *Schutzimpfungen selbst verantwortet. Gundlagen für eigene Entscheidungen*. Verlag Freies Geistesleben, Stuttgart 2004.
88. *Rilke's Book of Hours*. Tr. by Anita Barrows and Joanna Macy. US: Riverhead books 2004.
89. *Bible*. Revelation 14, 13.
90. Angelus Silesius.
91. See John 3: 1–8.
92. Bock E., *Wiederholte Erdenleben. Die Wiederverkörperungsidee der deutschen Geistesgeschichte*. Verlag Urachhaus, Stuttgart 1996.
93. Matthew 5: 1–7, 29.
94. Novalis, *Henry of Ofterdingen*, trans. Palmer Hilty, Waveland Press, 1990.
95. Steiner R. Various translations entitled *The Philosophy of Freedom. The Philosophy of Spiritual Activity. Intuitive Thinking as a Spiritual Path*. CW 4.
96. Steiner R. Various translations. *Theosophy*. CW 9.
97. Morgenstern C., *Stuttgarter Ausgabe*. Band 2 Lyrik 1906–1914. Urachhaus Verlag, Stuttgart 1992, S. 217.
98. Steiner R., Meuss A R., *Physiology and Healing*. CW 314. Lecture of 7 April 1920. Forest Row: Rudolf Steiner Press 2013.
99. See also: Waldorfpädagogik und Anthroposophische Medizin. Schwerpunktheft *Der Merkurstab* 4: 2012.
100. Steiner R., von Arnim C., *Understanding Healing*. CW 316. Forest Row: Rudolf Steiner Press 2013.
101. Loc. cit. First Newsletter. 11 March 1924. Medical Section of the School of Spiritual Science at the Goetheanum for the anthroposophical physicians and medical students.
102. Steiner R., Everett R., *The Renewal of Education*. CW 301. Kolisko Archive Publs for Steiner Schools Fellowship 1981.
103. Wiechert C., *Die Waldorfschule: Eine Einführung*. Verlag am Goetheanum, Dornach 2014.
104. Ruf B., *Trümmer und Traumata. Anthroposophische Grundlagen notfallpädagogischer Einsätze*. Verlag des Ita Wegman Instituts, Arlesheim 2012. Siehe auch unter: www.freunde-waldorf.de/notfallpaedagogik.html.

105. Literature on theory of the senses includes Steiner R., Creeger C E., Hardorp D., *Anthroposophy (A Fragment)*. CW 45.—Steiner R., Logan J F., *The Riddle of Humanity. The Spiritual Background of Human History*. Lecture of 12 August 1916.—Steiner R., *Von Seelenrätseln*. CW 21. IV/5: Über die wirkliche Grundlage der internationalen Beziehung.
106. As Note 10.
107. Spitzer M., *Digitale Demenz. Wie wir uns und unsere Kinder um den Verstand bringen*. Droemer Verlag, München 2012.
108. Steiner R., *Zur Sinneslehre*. Themen aus dem Gesamtwerk Bd. 3. Verlag Freies Geistesleben, Stuttgart 2014.
109. Auer W-G. *Sinnes-Welten*. Kösel Verlag, München 2007.
110. Grimm R., Kaschubowski (Hg.). *Kompendium der anthroposophischen Heilpädagogik*. Ernst Reinhardt Verlag, München 2008.
111. Glöckler M., Ethik des Sterbens und Würde des Lebens—Versuch einer anthroposophischen Stellungnahme zum assistierten Suizid. *Der Merkurstab* 2010, 5: 408–420.
112. Glöckler M., Heine R (Hg.) *Spiritualität im medizinischen Alltag: Sinnfragen beim Sterben von Kindern und alten Menschen*. Medizinische Sektion am Goetheanum, Dornach 2007.
113. Glöckler M., Heine R (Hg.). *Ethik des Sterbens—Würde des Lebens*. Verlag am Goetheanum, Dornach ^{2}2006.
114. Glöckler M., Heine R (Hg.). *Handeln im Umkreis des Todes*. Verlag am Goetheanum, Dornach ^{2}2003.
115. Arbeitskreis Anthroposophische Palliativmedizin in der Gesellschaft Anthroposophischer Ärzte (GAÄD), see also: http://www.gaed.de/gaaed/struktur/struktur/arbeitskreise-nach-fachrichtungen.html.
116. Glöckler M., Urteilskompeten und Entscheidungsfindung im Kontext von Hirntod und Organtransplantation. *Der Merkurstab* 5: 391–399, 2015.
117. Siehe zur In-Vitro-Fertilisation auch Michaela Glöckler (Hg.): *Medizin an der Schwelle*. Kap. Zum Schwangerschaftsabbruch. Verlag am Goetheanum, Dornach 1993, S. 40–45.
118. See Note 113.
119. Ibid.
120. Prokofieff S O., Selg P., *Das Leben schützen—Ärztliche Ethik und Suizidhilfe. Eine Betrachtung aus anthroposophischer Sicht*. Verlag am Goetheanum, Dornach ^{2}2016.

121. For further information see: http://www.individuelle-impfentscheidung.de/.

122. Goebel W., *Schutzimpfungen selbst verantwortet: Grundlagen für eigene Entscheidungen*. Verlag Freies Geistesleben, Stuttgart ^{4}2009.

123. Hirte M. Impfen—Pro & Contra. Droemersche Verlagsanstalt, München 2005.

124. Vagedes J., Soldner G., Vorsorgen und Impfen In: *Das Kindergesundheitsbuch*. Gräfe & Unzer Verlag, München, Neuausg. 2008.

125. Hildebrandt G., Physiologische Grundlagen der Hygiogenese. In: Heusser P (Hg.): *Akademische Forschung in der Anthroposophischen Medizin*. Beispiel: Hygiogenese. Natur- und geisteswissenschaftliche Zugänge zur Selbstheilungskraft des Menschen. Peter Lang Verlag, Bern 1999.

126. Antonovsky A., *Health, Strength and Coping* and other titles.

127. Opp G., Fingerle M (Hg.): *Was Kinder stärkt. Erziehung zwischen Risiko und Resilienz*. Ernst Reinhardt Verlag, München ^{3}2008.

128. Steiner R., *Ritualtexte für die Feiern des freien christlichen Religionsunterrichtes*. GA 269. Rudolf Steiner Verlag, Dornach 1997, S. 42–44.

129. von Goethe, J W., *West-östlicher Divan*. Insel Verlag, Berlin 2010.

130. Maslow A H., *Motivation and Personality*. Pearson ^{3}1997.

131. Frankl V E., *Logotherapie und Existenzanalyse: Texte aus sechs Jahrzehnten*. Beltz Verlag, Weinheim ^{3}2010.

132. Fuchs T., *Das Gehirn—Ein Beziehungsorgan: Eine Phänomenologisch-Ökologische Konzeption*. Kohlhammer Verlag, Stuttgart 2007. *Ecology of the Brain: The phenomenology and biology of the embodied mind* (International Perspectives in Philosophy and Psychiatry). OUP Oxford 2017.

133. Buehler W, Maloney L., *Living with Your Body*. Rudolf Steiner Press 1979.

134. Gesellschaft Anthroposophischer Ärzte in Deutschland (GAÄD) und Medizinische Sektion am Goetheanum (Hg.): *Vademecum anthroposophische Arzneimittel*. Dornach ^{3}2013.

135. As Note 7.

136. Meyer U., Petersen P A (ed.). *Anthroposophische Pharmazie. Grundlagen, Herstellprozesse, Arzneimittel*. Salumed Verlag, Berlin 2016.

137. Zur anthroposophischen Veterinärmedizin siehe Spranger J., *Lehrbuch der anthroposophischen Tiermedizin*. Sonntag Verlag, Stuttgart 2006.

138. International Association of Anthroposophic Pharmacists IAAP: *Anthroposophic Pharmaceutical Codex*. Wissenschaftliche Verlagsgesellschaft Stuttgart, Stuttgart 2014.
139. See also Girke M., *Innere Medizin. Grundlagen und therapeutische Konzepte der Anthroposophischen Medizin*. Kap. VIII. Salumed Verlag, Berlin 2011.
140. Husemann F., Zum Wesensgliedergefüge der Hypertonie. *Der Merkurstab* 1990, 2: 116–117.
141. As Note 134.
142. Kusserow M., Äussere Anwendungen in der anthroposophisch erweiterten Medizin. *Weleda Korrespondenzblätter für Ärzte* 1992, 133 : 122–153.
143. Steiner R., Parker A H., Gates J., Bamford C., *The Effects of Esoteric/Occult Development*. CW 145. Hudson: Anthroposophic Press 1997.
144. Ulbricht R L., Coronary heart disease: seven dietary factors. Southgate DA1991, *Lancet* 338: 985–992.
145. Appel L J., Moore R J., Obarzanek E et al. For the DASH Collaborative Research Group. A clinical trial of the effects of dietary patterns on blood pressure. *New English Journal of Medicine* 1997, 336: 1117–1124.
146. Eaton S B., Korner N. Palleo Nutrion: A consideration of its nature and implications. *New Engl. Journal of Medicine* 1987: 312.
147. As Note 49.
148. Klaus D., Böhm M., Halle M., Kolloch R., Mideke M., Pavenstädt H., Hoyer J., Die Beschränkung der Kochsalzaufnahme in der Gesamtbevölkerung verspricht langfristig grossen Nutzen. *Dtsch Med Wochenschr* 2009, 134: 108–118.
149. Cook N R., Obarzanek E., Cutler J A., Billing J E., Rexrode K M., Kumanyika S K., Appel U., Whelton P K., Trials of Hypertension Prevention Collaborative Research Group: Joint effects of sodium and potassium intake on subsequent cardiovascular disease. The trials of hypertension prevention follow-up study. *Arch Intern Med* 2009, 169: 32–40.
150. Barbagallo M., Dominguez L J., Galioto A., Ferlisi A., Cani C., Malfa L., Pineo A., Busando A., Paolisso G., Role of magnesium in insulin action, diabetes and cardiometabolic syndrome x. *Molecular Aspects of Medicine* 2003, 24: 39–52.
151. Miyachi M., Kawano H., Sugawara J., Takahashi K., Hayashi K., Yamazaki K., Tabata I., Tanaka H., Unfavourable effects of resistance

training on central arterial compliance. *Circulation* 2001, 110: 2858–2863.
152. Hambrecht R. et al. Effect of exercise on coronary endothelial function in patients with coronary artery disease. *New Engl. Journal of Medicine* 2000, 342: 454–460.
153. As Note 28.
154. Trenkwalder P., Kognitive Störungen und Demenz—neue Endorganschäden bei Hypertonie. *Dtsch. Med. Wschr* 2000, 115: 1349.
155. As Note 21.
156. Rissmann W., Unipolare depressive Störungen. As in Note 7.
157. See also Soldner G., Stellmann H M., Otitis media. In *Individuelle Pädiatrie*. Wissenschaftliche Verlagsgesellschaft, Stuttgart 2011.
158. Vgl. u.a. Sommer M. Behandlung der Otitis media ohne Antibiotika. *Der Merkurstab* 51: 373–374, 1998.
159. Lange P., in Note 56.
160. See also Lange P., *Hausmittel für Kinder. Natürlich vorbeugen und heilen*. Rowohlt, Reinbek 2012.
161. As Note 5.
162. Kühne P., Anthroposophische Ernährung. Lebensmittel und ihre Qualität. Arbeitskreis für Ernährungsforschung, Bad Vilbel 2008, siehe auch http://www.ak-ernaehrung.de/.
163. Kühne P., Anthroposophische Ernährung II—Mineralstoffe und Spurenelemente. Arbeitskreis für Ernährungsforschung, Bad Vilbel 2008, siehe auch http://www.ak-ernaehrung.de/.
164. Steiner R., *Ernährung und Bewusstsein*. Verlag Freies Geistesleben Stuttgart 2014.
165. As Note 47.
166. Matthew 4: 4. Kalmia Bittleston translation.
167. kontakt@lebensgemeinschaft-bingenheim.de.
168. Aus Morgenstern C., *Wir fanden einen Pfad*. Rudolf Steiner Verlag, Dornach 2004.
169. Steiner R., *Vom Lebenslauf des Menschen*. Themen aus dem Gesamtwerk Band 4, hg. von Fucke E. Verlag Freies Geistesleben, Stuttgart [6]2006.
170. Steiner R., *Stichwort Karma*. Futurum Verlag, Basel 2013.
171. Lievegoed B., Cornelius. J M., *Man on the Threshold*. Hawthorn Press 1985.
172. Treichler R., Meuss A., *Soulways: The Developing Soul-life Phases, Thresholds and Biography*. Hawthorn Press 1996.

173. More information on website of Deutsche Gesellschaft für Anthroposophische Psychotherapie e.V.: http://www.anthroposophische-psychotherapie.de.
174. Siehe z.B. Burkhard G., *Das Leben in die Hand nehmen*. Verlag Freies Geistesleben, Stuttgart [16]2014. Dies.: *Schlüsselfragen zur Biografie*. Verlag Freies Geistesleben, Stuttgart [10]2013. Hanses A (Hg.) *Biographie und Soziale Arbeit*. Schneider Hohengehren, München 2004. Lievegoed B., *Lebenskrisen—Lebenschancen*. Kösel Verlag, München [12]2001. Wais M., *Biographiearbeit—Lebensberatung*. Verlag Urachhaus, Stuttgart [7]2010.
175. Dekkers A., O'Sullivan A., *Psychology of Human Dignity*.
176. Kienle G S., *Der sogenannte Placebo-Effekt: Illusion—Fakten—Realität*. Schattauer Verlag, Stuttgart 1995.
177. For up-to-date information see http://www.icaat-medsektion.net/.
178. Marie Steiner's Introduction to *Art as Seen in the Light of Mystery Wisdom*. CW 275.
179. Rittelmeyer C., *Schulbauten positiv gestalten. Wie Schüler Farben und Formen erleben*. Bauverlag, Wiesbaden 1994.
180. See also Fäth R., *Die therapeutische Dimension von Architektur und Design*. Pforte Verlag, Dornach 2007.
181. Raab R., Klingborg A., *Die Waldorfschule baut: 60 Jahre Architektur der Waldorfschule*. Verlag Freies Geistesleben Stuttgart 1982.
182. Rittelmeyer C., *Einführung in die Gestaltung von Schulbauten. Ein Lehr- und Schulungsbuch*. Verlag Farbe und Gesundheit, Frammersbach 2013.
183. De Ris Allen J., *Living Buildings. An Expression of Fifty Years of Camphill, Halls and Chapels of the Camphill Movement*. Bieldside, Aberdeen 1990.
184. Golombek E., Plastisch-therapeutisches Gestalten. Anthroposophische Kunsttherapie Bd 1. Urachhaus Verlag Stuttgart [2]2003.
185. Siehe dazu: ritabaumgart-kunsttherapie.de/praxis.html.
186. da Vinci L., MacCurdy., *Notebooks of Leonardo da Vinci*. Folio Society.
187. Steiner R., Stockton A., rev. von Arnim C., *Art*. Lecture of 28 Oct. 1909 from CW 271.
188. Mees-Christeller E., Denzinger I., Altmaier M et al. Therapeutisches Zeichnen und Malen. *Anthroposophische Kunsttherapie* Bd 2. Urachhaus Verlag, Stuttgart [2]2002.
189. Altmaier M., *Der kunsttherapeutische Prozess*. Verlag Urachhaus, Stuttgart 1995.

190. Steiner R., St Goar M., *The Inner Nature of Music*. From CW 283. New York: Anthroposophic Press 1983.
191. Felber R., Reinhold S., Musiktherapie und Gesang. *Anthroposophische Kunsttherapie* Bd 3. Verlag Urachhaus, Stuttgart [2]2003.
192. Beilharz G (Hg.) *Musik in Pädagogik und Therapie*. Verlag Freies Geistesleben, Stuttgart 2004.
193. See also Brown L S., Jellison J A., Music research with children and youth with disabilities and typically developing peers: a systematic review. *Journal of Music Therapy* 2012; 49 (3): 335–364.
194. See also Gold C., Moessler K., Grocke D et al. Individual music therapy for mental health care clients with low therapy motivation: multicentre randomised controlled trial. *Psychotherapy and Psychosomatics* 2013; 82 (5): 319–331.
195. See also Tillmann B., Music and language perception: expectations, structural integration, and cognitive sequencing. *Topics in Cognitive Science* 2012; 4 (4): 568–584.
196. Werbeck-Svaerdstroem V., Luborsky P., *Uncovering the Voice. The Cleansing Power of Song*. Rudolf Steiner Press 2008.
197. See also: http://www.schule-der-stimmenthuellung.de/.
198. See also: Medizinische Sektion am Goetheanum (Hg.): *Meditationen zur Herztätigkeit gegeben von Rudolf Steiner*. Dornach [2]2014.
199. Steiner R., *Mantrische Sprüche. Seelenübungen II*. GA 268. Rudolf Steiner Verlag, Dornach 1999, S. 181.
200. Ibid., S. 179.
201. Steiner R., Adams M., *Speech and Drama*. CW 282. London: Anthroposophical Publishing Co. 1960.
202. Von Bonin D., *Materialien zur Therapeutischen Sprachgestaltung*. Verlag am Goetheanum, Dornach 2009.
203. Slezak-Schindler C., *Sprachanbahnung—Sprechfreude*. Marie Steiner Verlag, Unterlengenhardt 2009.
204. For up-to-date information see http://heileurythmie-medsektion.net/de/heileurythmie.
205. Sam M M., *Eurythmie: Entstehungsgeschichte und Porträts ihrer Pioniere*. Verlag am Goetheanum, Dornach 2014.
206. Hachtel B., Gäch A., *Bibliographie Heileurythmie. Veröffentlichungen von 1920–2005*. Verlag Natur-Mensch-Medizin, Bad Boll 2007.
207. Weitere Forschungsergebnisse unter: http://heileurythmie-medsektion.net/de/tr/forschung.

208. Steiner R., Compton-Burnett V & J., Dubrovik S & C., *Eurythmy as Visible Speech*. CW 279. Lecture of 10 July 1924. London: Anthroposophical Publishing Co. 1956.
209. Patzlaff R (Hg.) *Luftlautformen sichtbar gemacht*. Verlag Freies Geistesleben, Stuttgart ^{2}2003.
210. As Note 5.
211. For further information see http://www.medsektion-goetheanum.org/home/fachbereichekoordinationderarbeitsfelder/pflege/.
212. Heine R., Bay F., *Anthroposophische Pflegepraxis. Pflege als Gestaltungsaufgabe*. Hippokrates Verlag, Stuttgart ^{2}2003.
213. Heine R., Die pflegerische Geste. Ein Konzept der anthroposophischen Pflege. In: *Dr Mabuse. Zeitschrift für alle Gesundheitsberufe*. Jahrgang 170: 30–33, 2007.
214. Fingado M., Therkleson T & S., *Compresses and Other Therapeutic Applications. A Handbook from the Ita Wegman Clinic*. Floris Books 2012.
215. Layer M., *Praxishandbuch Rhythmische Einreibungen nach Wegman/Hauschka*. Verlag Hans Huber, Bern ^{2}2014.
216. WALA (Hg.). *Jungebad*. Kostenlose Broschüre zum Download: http://www.walaarzneimittel.de/ratgeber/pdf/Jungebad-Broschuere.pdf.
217. Batschko E M., Dengler S., *Praxisbuch der Rhythmischen Massage* nach Ita Wegman. Info3 Verlag, Frankfurt 2011.
218. Hauschka M., *Rhythmische Massage nach Dr Ita Wegman: Menschenkundliche Grundlagen*. Verein zur Förderung der Künstlerischen Therapie und Massage, Bad Boll 1972.
219. Pressel S., *Bewegung ist Heilung*. Verlag Freies Geistesleben, Stuttgart 2007.
220. https://www.oelundwasser.de/.
221. von Bothmer A., *Die Bothmer-Gymnastik: Pädagogische und therapeutische Anwendungsmöglichkeiten*. Stuttgart: Schattauer Verlag 2004.
222. McMillan J., *Still Moving: Image and Imagination*. Spacial Dynamics Institute, Schuylerville, NY 2015.
223. For further information see http://www.khsdornach.org/.
224. Selg P., *The Therapeutic Eye. How Rudolf Steiner Observed Children*. SteinerBooks 2003.
225. van Zabern B., *Kompendium der ärztlichen Behandlung seelenpflegebedürftiger Kinder, Jugendlicher und Erwachsener. Erfahrung*

und Hinweise aus der anthroposophischen Therapie. Verlag am Goetheanum, Dornach 2002.
226. Grimm R., *Bibliographie der anthroposophischen Heilpädagogik und Sozialtherapie*. Verlag am Goetheanum, Dornach 1993.
227. Bloomard P., *Beziehungsgestaltung in der Begleitung von Menschen mit Behinderungen. Aspekte der Berufsethik der Heilpädagogik und Sozialtherapie*. Athena-Verlag, Oberhausen 2012.
228. Frielingsdorf V., Grimm R., Kaldenberg B., *Die Geschichte der anthroposophischen Heilpädagogik und Sozialtherapie. Entwicklungslinien und Aufgabenfelder 1920–1980*. Verlag am Goetheanum, Dornach 2013.
229. Koenig K., Selg P., Author of translation not stated. *The child with special needs: Letters and essays*. Floris Books.
230. Beauftragte der Bundesregierung für die Belange behinderter Menschen (Hg.) *Die UN-Behindertenrechtskonvention. Übereinkommen über die Rechte von Menschen mit Behinderungen vom 13. Dezember 2006*. Präambel, Absatz m.
231. Barth U., Maschke R., *Inklusion—Vielfalt gestalten: Ein Praxisbuch*. Verlag Freies Geistesleben, Stuttgart 2014.
232. Kiene H., Komplementäre Methodenlehre der klinischen Forschung. *Cognition based Medicine*, Springer Verlag, Berlin/Heidelberg 2001.
233. See http://www.ifaemm.de/.
234. Kienle G S., Kiene H., *Die Mistel in der Onkologie—Fakten und konzeptionelle Grundlagen*. Schattauer Verlag, Stuttgart 2003.
235. Tröger W., Galun D., Reif M., Schmann A., Stanković N., Milićević M., Lebensqualität von Menschen mit fortgeschrittenem Pankreaskarzimon unter Misteltherapie. *Deutsches Ärzteblatt* 29–30: 493–502, 2014.
236. Matthes H., Beurteilung von Arzneimittelindikationen, -sicherheit, -wirksamkeit und –nutzen in der konventionellen und komplementären Medizin unter spezieller Berücksichtigung der Anthroposophischen Medizin mittels eines elektronischen Ärztenetzwerkes (EvaMed). Habilitationsschrift. Medizinische Fakultät Charité, Universitätsmedizin, Berlin 2011.
237. Siehe Publikationsliste: www.uni-wh.de/universitaet/personen verzeichnis/details/show/Employee/heusser/.
238. Self P., *Gerhard Kienle: Leben und Werk*. 2 Bde. Verlag am Goetheanum, Dornach 2003.

239. Kienle G., *Arzneimittelsicherheit und Gesellschaft*. Schattauer Verlag, Stuttgart 1974.
240. See www.medsektion-goetheanum.org/forschung.
241. See also Girke M., Matthiessen P (Hg.) *Dialogforum Pluralismus in der Medizin: Medizin und Menschenbild*. Bad Homburg 2015.
242. The lecture presentations are on the congress website: http://www.icihm.org/de/praesentationen.html.

Further Reading

Victor Bott, *An Introduction to Anthroposophical Medicine, Extending the Art of Healing*

Sergio Maria Francardo, *Anthroposophic Medicine for all the Family, Recognizing and Treating the Most Common Disorders*

Ross Rentea, Mark Kamsler and Andrea Rentea, *Childhood Illnesses and Immunization, Anthroposophic Ideas to Ensure the Wellbeing of our Children in this Digital Age*

Walther Bühler, *Living With Your Body, Health, Illness and Understanding the Human Being*

By Rudolf Steiner:

With Dr Ita Wegman, *Extending Practical Medicine, Fundamental Principles Based on the Science of the Spirit*

Introducing Anthroposophical Medicine

The Healing Process, Spirit, Nature and our Bodies

Illness and Therapy, Spiritual-Scientific Aspects of Healing

Understanding Healing, Meditative Reflections on Deepening Medicine through Spiritual Science

Information on Anthroposophic Medicine

Useful information on anthroposophic medicine worldwide can be found at the website of the Medical Section of the School of Spiritual Science at the Goetheanum:
www.medsektion-goetheanum.org

The Medical Section is the hub of the whole anthroposophic medical movement. Fundamentally, it provides:

- post-graduate medical specialisation;
- training of paramedical staff;
- coordination of educational and research activities.

The body coordinating the individual medical associations is the International Federation of Anthroposophic Medical Associations (IVAA):
www.ivaa.info

General Anthroposophical Society

For more general information on anthroposophy and on the General Anthroposophical Society, visit or contact:
www.goetheanum.org
sekretariat@goetheanum.org
Address:
General Anthroposophical Society
Rüttiweg 45
CH-4143 Dornach 1
Switzerland
Tel. +41 (0)61 706 42 42